IEE COMPUTING SERIES 20

Series Editors: Dr. B. A. Carré
Dr. D. A. H. Jacobs

VIRTUAL REALITY
IN ENGINEERING

VIRTUAL REALITY
IN ENGINEERING

**Edited by
Kevin Warwick, John Gray
and David Roberts**

The Institution of Electrical Engineers

Published by: The Institution of Electrical Engineers, London, United Kingdom

© 1993: The Institution of Electrical Engineers

The Institution of Electrical Engineers,
Michael Faraday House,
Six Hills Way, Stevenage,
Herts. SG1 2AY, United Kingdom

British Library Cataloguing in Publication Data

A CIP catalogue record for this book
is available from the British Library

ISBN 0 85296 803 5

Printed in England by Short Run Press Ltd., Exeter

Contents

Contributors

I. Andrew
Dimension International
Zephyr One
Calleva Park
Aldermaston, RG7 4QZ.

C. Bridgewater
Dept. of Civil Engineering
Imperial College of Science
 Technology and Medicine
South Kensington
London SW7 2BT.

P. duPont
Division Limited
19 Apex Court
Woodlands Almondsbury
Bristol BS12 4JT

R. Gallery
Philips Research Laborotories
Cross Oak Lane
Redhill RH1 5HA.

I. Gibson
Dept. Manufacturing Eng.
 & Operation Management
Faculty of Engineering
University Park
Nottingham, NG7 2RD.

J. Gray
Dept. of Electronic &
 Electrical Engineering
University of Salford
Salford M54WT.

M. Griffin
Cybernetics Virtual Reality
 Research Group
School of Engineering and
 Information Sciences
University of Reading
PO BOX 225
Whiteknights
Reading RG6 2AY.

D. Harrison
School of Systems Engineering
University of Portsmouth
Anglesea Building
Anglesea Road
Portsmouth, PO1 3DJ.

M. Hartshorn
Dept. of Chemistry
University of York
Heslington, York Y01 5DD

T. Howe
Heathrow House (S518)
British Airways
PO BOX 35
Hounslow, TW6 9RS.

P. Jackson
Advanced Systems Dept.
Military Systems Division
Link Miles Ltd.
Churchill Industrial Estate
Lancing BN15 8UE

D. Roberts
Cybernetics Virtual Reality
 Research Group
School of Engineering and
 Information Sciences
University of Reading
PO BOX 225
Whiteknights
Reading RG6 2AY.

R. Stone
The National Advanced
 Robotics Research Centre
University Road
Salford M5 4PP.

K. Warwick
Dept. of Cybernetics
School of Engineering
 and Information Sciences
University of Reading
PO BOX 225, Whiteknights
Reading RG6 2AY.

W. Webster
BNF
Building 48
Selerfield
Sea Scale
Cumbria LA20 1PG.

Acknowledgements

The editors would like to thank all of the authors for their contributions and their promptness in forwarding their chapters for final preparation. Thanks are also given to Paul Sandoz, Ian Rawlings, Louise Martin and Richard Mitchell for their assistance in editing the chapters, Mike Griffin as technical editor, Phillip Stokes for philosophical advice, Deborah Pope for artwork and Lynne Griffin for P.A.

On behalf of all the authors, the editors would like to thank those at the IEE who were responsible for the production of this book and workshop organisation, in particular Fiona MacDonald and John St. Aubyn for the former and David Penrose for the latter. Thanks must also go to Pierre duPont of Division limited who gave much assistance in the initial planning.

August 1993   K. Warwick
                                                     J. O. Gray
                                                     D. Roberts

Preface

The intention of this book is to provide an introduction to the techniques involved in the design and development of virtual reality systems. The book is aimed primarily at engineers and engineering students who have a basic knowledge of computer hardware and software and wish to become more widely informed about the overall virtual reality area. Owing to the nature of the content, it will however be of considerable interest to managers and others with a business background who would like to gain an insight into the topic. It must be emphasised that what follows is concerned with giving a broad look at the subject rather than putting forward detailed descriptions of a technical nature or, on the other hand, abstract theoretical ideas. Indeed the book is based on an IEE vacation school, held at the University of Reading, and provides a balanced perspective of the theme of virtual reality in engineering. It may therefore be used as a source of reference or could form the basis of a university-based course on virtual reality.

Virtual reality has developed into a practical, useful entity over the last few years due partly to the availability of faster and more advanced computer hardware and partly to the requirements of end users. It has grown into an exciting field which has already seen the development of numerous and diverse application areas, from rehabilitation of the handicapped to monitoring and management of large financial markets. It is now felt timely to evaluate current developments in the technology so that new achievements can build progressively and cohesively from a solid base. The object of this book is to present the advances in virtual reality in a readily digestible way by linking theoretical developments with practical implementations. A feature of the book is the inclusion of material from a wide range of manufacturers in the virtual reality area which aims to demonstrate the available technology. The overall tutorial nature of the academic-based contributions then provides a balance in order to give a general introduction.

Chapter 1

An overview of virtual reality

D. Roberts and K. Warwick

"We may observe, that it is universally allowed by
philosophers, and is besides pretty obvious of itself,
that nothing is ever really present to the mind but its
perceptions or impressions and ideas, and that
external objects become known to us only by their
perceptions they occasion. To hate, to love, to think, to
feel, to see: all this is nothing but to perceive"

[HUME39]

In this chapter, a broad introduction is given to the field of virtual reality. Obviously as a starting pointing, the question can be asked: "What is virtual reality?" The philosophical rationale of the technology is discussed in Section 1.1 by showing that knowledge can be increased by making possible the perception of new principles. A tighter definition of the technology is also given in terms of computer generated models and human–computer interaction, wherein immersive and desktop approaches are compared. A typical system is described which demonstrates that a virtual workstation can be constructed with a relatively low budget and the section finishes by discussing some important factors that have to be overcome to facilitate effective human/computer interaction in virtual reality.

Virtual environments can be used to bring physically remote people together, hence section 1.2: "Multi-user environments", discusses computer assisted co-operative working and how virtual reality is an ideal base for tele-working.

Virtual environments need not be completely abstract, they can act as a crystal ball looking into and even affecting reality itself, in section 1.3 it is therefore demonstrated, with an example application, how virtual reality can be used to visualise and manage a large system.

Many commercial applications have already been developed, hence in section 1.4, a number of practical examples are introduced and it is shown that virtual reality can be used for anything from rehabilitating the handicapped to monitoring the stock market or training pilots. An overall conclusion from the chapter is that virtual reality is not "Blue sky research" and can be applied to many engineering problems.

1.1   What is virtual reality ?

It has been argued by many philosophers that reality is not a set of physical objects that we perceive in a certain way, but instead that reality is purely what we perceive. George Berkeley considered that matter did not exist and that all that was real was sensation [GRIFF91]. He further believed that the perceptions themselves were maintained by the mind of his god. This can be considered analogous to a virtual environment maintained by a central entity, the computer, perceived by man. Although this gives credence to the use of the term virtual reality, it does not promote its usefulness. Knowledge within the human framework can be considered in terms of "justified true belief" [ADDI85]. Belief is gained through perception, thus both knowledge and thought can be qualified as derivatives of perception. David Hume once wrote:

> "Now since nothing is ever present to the mind but
> perceptions ... it follows that it is impossible for us to
> so much as conceive or form an idea of anything
> specifically different from ideas and impressions. Let
> us fix our attention out of ourselves as much as
> possible; let us chase our imagination to the heavens,
> or to the utmost limits of the universe; we never really
> advance a step beyond ourselves, nor can conceive any
> kind of existence, but these perceptions which have
> appeared in that narrow compass. This is the
> universe of the imagination, nor have we any idea but
> what is there produced"
>
> [HUME39]

If our overall level of perception can be increased this should result in a greater "universe of imagination".

The human sensory system has evolved to interpret information that we once needed for survival. Today our survival requirements are very different. We now require different information, for example, the trends of the stock market, to be interpreted. It is only possible to comprehend in terms of what we have perceived, so abstract information that cannot be perceived through our senses, must be metamorphosed so that it can.

"The perceptual senses are faculties for acquisition of knowledge about what is currently perceptible in one's environment. To perceive is to apprehend, discern, observe, recognise or distinguish some current feature of one's sensory organs"

[HACK87]

Virtual reality allows us to map information gained from man-made sensors, or other information sources, to our own well developed sensory organs. For example, a map created from a radar can be recreated in three-dimensional space surrounding an observer. Using tactile feedback gloves, the observer could even touch and feel the virtual landscape.

1.1.1 A definition of virtual reality

Virtual reality can be described as the science of integrating man with information. It consists of three-dimensional, interactive, computer generated environments. These environments can be models of real or imaginary worlds. Their purpose is to represent information through synthetic experience. Conceptualisation of complex or abstract systems is made possible by representing their components as symbols that give powerful sensory cues, related in some way to their meaning. Virtual reality incorporates much human aspects engineering which maximises its impact on the senses and therefore the perception of the individual. The technology was born from the merging of many disciplines including psychology, cybernetics, computer graphics, database design, real-time and distributed systems, electronics, robotics, multimedia and telepresence.

Figure 1.1   *A typical immersive system*
Courtesy of Division Limited

A virtual model differs from that produced by, say, a CAD system in two basic ways. Firstly, the objects, some of which represent the users, can interact. For example, a person can pick up a torch and switch it on. Secondly, behaviours can be associated with objects; for example, a cat can chase a mouse. The model itself may represent a system in the real world and affect and can be affected by that system through control and monitoring devices.

Immersive virtual reality uses output devices designed to map as directly as possible to the user's perceptual organs, see Figure 1.1. A head-mounted display (HMD) encases the audio and visual perception of the user in the virtual environment and cuts out all outside information. Head and body tracking moves the user about the world and interaction with objects is monitored by sensing devices on the hands.

Desktop virtual reality uses conventional computer input and output devices such as a keyboard, mouse and monitor, see Figure 1.2. Although this does not give the same level of spatial awareness as its immersive counterpart, it does offer a more traditional approach and does not require the user to wear a head-mounted display. This has been found an attractive compromise by many end users uncertain about spending long periods of time in a headset.

Figure 1.2   *A typical desktop system*
Courtesy of Dimension International

1.1.2 Where did it begin ?

In 1965 Ivan Sutherland presented a paper "The ultimate display" [SUTH65]. This described the concept of a head-mounted display system. In this paper Sutherland stated that the illusion presented to the user should "look real, act real, sound real, feel real". Three years later he demonstrated the first ever working head-mounted display [SUTH68]. The display was connected via a series of mechanical arms to the ceiling. The stretch of each joint in this linkage was monitored by a potentiometer allowing the position and orientation of the users head to be calculated. Computer graphics, at this time one of the main driving forces in this area, was still using graph plotters for high definition pictures. It was not until the next decade that raster based systems became common place.

1.1.3 A typical system

A typical virtual reality system may be based around a micro-computer, for example a PC. Such a machine, incorporating a graphics accelerator, would produce up to 10,000 polygons a second. These polygons can be covered by a texture map or a digitised image to give a realistic image. A head-mounted display consisting of two small LCD TV screens with a lens or perhaps mirror assembly provides the user with the visual stimulus. The pictures displayed on each screen are slightly offset to provide the correct parallax and give an idea of depth. A magnetic or infra-red tracking system monitors the position and orientation of the operator's head and hands. As the user turns, the panorama swings but the 3-D sound, supplied through earphones, appears to be locked to its source. The hand of the user, covered by a gesture sensing glove, allows interaction with the virtual world. To allow entry into numerous worlds and interaction with other users, the computer can be networked over communication channels such as Internet.

1.1.4 Human and computer considerations

Interaction between a human and a virtual environment can be regarded as a closed loop system [MOSH93][HOFS79]. The Virtual Environment is perceived by the human who then alters it. This change of state is reflected back to the human who may alter it again and the cycle continues. In such a relationship both parties must provide the services required by the other. As the virtual environment exists for the benefit of the human, it may be considered that the environment should be expected to make more compromises.

An important aim of any virtual reality system is to give a natural feel to the illusion. The visual and audio resolution should match that perceivable by the user. With present LCD technology it is difficult to produce a display that, when held close to the eyes, does not show the individual pixels. One method of overcoming this is to place a film of microlenses over the screen [CVRRG]. Each microlens diffuses and mixes the discrete colours from a tri-pixel (red, green and blue LCD set) to give a single colour. This removes the perceived pixellation but does not increase the screen resolution.

Another important problem is latency. Latency is the measure of the delay between a cause of a state change to the virtual environment and the subsequent update and display of the effect. This delay is caused by the work required by the computer to observe the cause, calculate the change and display the new state. A system is said to be realtime if it can guarantee a set maximum latency for all given tasks. A hard realtime system is one that will take the action necessary to ensure the maximum latency is not exceeded even if this means ignoring information. In virtual reality the latency of the system must be less than that perceivable by a human being. For example, a person moving their arm would expect to see their virtual arm moving at the same speed. Latency is related to the complexity of the model. To make such a system hard real time, an algorithm can be employed that calculates how long it will take to update the model and display. If this time will cause the latency to increase over a set limit, the algorithm will reduce the complexity of the model by an order necessary to meet the deadline.

1.1.5   Latest developments

The concept of people sitting at home all day plugged into virtual reality is, to many, quite horrific. This is partly because of the state of current technology. At present, head-mounted display (HMD) systems are cumbersome and uncomfortable and give the impression to an onlooker that the user is wearing a box on their head. In the very near future, it is probable that HMDs will more closely resemble a pair of sun glasses. A recent breakthrough in display technology now allows a high definition colour image with a resolution similar to a typical television to be produced from a thin sheet of plastic. Full body tracking will be achievable through image processing. This could replace the data glove with reflective nail varnish.

It is now possible to purchase systems that detect nerve pulses by sensors strapped across the outer skin. It is claimed that eye tracking can be achieved by wearing a strap across the forehead and hand gesture recognition sensed from a wrist strap. The ultimate virtual reality system would be directly coupled to the nervous system, but this is a long way off.

As with most experiences, virtual reality is more enjoyable when shared. Much research is being conducted into large, multi user systems that will one day span the world.

1.2   Multi-user virtual reality

> *"Our notion of two things having the same colour,*
> *say, is only as secure as our ability to master an*
> *overwhelming majority who see them as having the*
> *same colour"*
>
> [BENN]

Teleworking: working from home and communicating with the outside world using telephone, fax and videoconferencing, is seen as a way of reintroducing prosperity to rural areas [GEAK93]. In May of 1993, a £1,000,000 teleworking centre was opened in West Wales and will hopefully provide work for 500 people. David Oborne at the University of Swansea has carried out a two year study into the psychological aspects of teleworking in rural areas (PATRA) in which he found that teleworking appears to have no adverse psychological effects on the individuals concerned.

There are many advantages to teleworking. Commuting is known to be one of the most stressful aspects of office life and it is not uncommon for people to spend over three hours a day commuting. Consider how many man hours are wasted each week by people travelling into and across the major metropolises. Indeed, since the bombing of the financial district of London earlier this year, much debate has been made about methods of decentralising the banks for security.

It has long been accepted that a team of people working together towards the same goal is much more productive than individuals working at discord. Computer assisted co-operative working allows teams of computer users to interact through their terminals, however, current computer interfaces do not encourage team work. Electronic mail, talk and bulletin boards only allow transfer of text which has a very low information content; "A single picture carries a thousand words". White boards allow a number of people on different terminals to write text in a window displayed to all users. However, the problem with white boards is that it is not intuitive which user is writing at a given instance. The Swedish Institute of Computer Science (SICS) has found that interaction on a white board is more intuitive if, using virtual reality, each member of the team is represented as a three-dimensional object which can point to, and write on, the board [CARL93]. These alter-egos need not be realistic "Cyber-droids" [CYBE92] but merely representations of where their real self is looking. For example, in SICS's distributed interactive virtual environment (DIVE), the users are represented by oblong or T-shaped objects with eyes on one side.

Distributed virtual reality allows people to interact in a true three-dimensional domain. Two people in different parts of the world could theoretically shake hands at the beginning of a virtual teleconference. There are very many things that cannot be adequately represented as a two-dimensional model. Take, for example, a building. A user could, without leaving their home, call up an estate agent on a virtual reality network, who would then show them around a full scale three-dimensional model of the property. The realism provided by virtual reality makes it practical to carry out many tasks from the comfort of the family home. A virtual market place or supermarket could offer goods to the consumer. A shopper could then walk up to a packet of biscuits and ask it about its own nutritional value. Advertising would no longer be restricted by problems of space. A virtual car show room for example, could offer breath-taking rides around a race track in their latest models. Supporting this kind of virtual "cyberspace" [GIBS84] would require the co-operation of many organisations. The network itself along with the support of virtual reality would be provided by a telecommunications company. Developers would buy the permission to set up virtual shopping centres and then sell the right to set up shops to retailers. Architects and graphic designers would offer shop designs and displays. Virtual advertising could lie and make something look better than it really is, therefore some form of policing would be required to enforce the laws of fair trade.

It has been shown how a parallel reality can be formed purely from information. It is not possible however, to support a society on data alone. Food still needs to be obtained and refuse disposed of. Links are necessary between the real and virtual world.

1.3 Interaction with reality

*"the things in sharpest focus are the things that are
public enough to be talked of publicly, common and
conspicuous enough to be talked of often, and near
enough to sense to be quickly identified and learned
by name."*

[QUIN60]

The models supported by virtual reality need not be abstract and can be representations of data from the real world. There are many large systems that are monitored and the data sent to a computer to aid management. British Telecom's telecommunication network, for example, has around 25,000,000 customer lines grouped by approximately 6,000 digital exchanges. Exchange and line loading information is gathered at an average rate of 1 Megabyte per second [REA93]. Although much of the network management is automated, there is still a large amount of decision-making carried out manually. To help manage this huge network, British Telecom are developing a virtual reality visualiser. A prototype, not yet linked to the real network, allows a user to fly around a 3-D model of the network and gain loading information at various nodes. The first view of the model is a silhouette of the British Isles on top of which are placed three vertically separated protocol layers: access, switch and transport, see Figure 3. At each level, cubes with interconnecting tubes represent network nodes and communication channels, respectively. A user can fly into any of the cubes and be presented with loading data in the form of pie charts. A fully developed system may receive and display information from the network in real time and facilitate interactive management.

Monitoring of information is becoming ever more efficient. Local operating networks (LONs) are networks of discrete silicon chips capable of monitoring, control and communication functions. Once programmed, LONs are able to control a complex system, for example an oil refinery, and send sensing information back to a conventional computer. On a network level, LONs have built into their hardware, the protocol (TCP/IP) required to be a member of an Internet. Such self-contained inexpensive networks offer huge potential for pumping data into and out of virtual models. Cameras are becoming very small and unobtrusive and, although image processing is still a long way from being perfected, its usability is rising quickly. David Gelernter [GELE91] suggests that the functionality of an entire city can be represented and interacted with through virtual reality. His book "Mirror Worlds: or the day software puts the universe in a shoe box... how it will happen and what it will mean", describes how traffic, commerce and any organisation can be monitored and mirrored on a computer. This book is not an unsubstantiated work of fiction. Gelernter actually explains in detail how such a system could be put together with existing technology.

If a parallel dimension is created in which we can experience far more and interact with whomever we choose, will we still require the same commodities? J.D. Foss of GPT believes that "Information is the most marketable commodity of the 1990s" [FOSS93]. He cites the need for brokers to act between the consumer and the owners of the information. Brokers, on behalf of the clients, would consult the various suppliers and obtain the required information at a competitive price. For the suppliers they could find buyers and handle charges. A client or perhaps a broker might decide to employ a number of agents to act as information collectors and refiners. These agents might be humans who interact with the virtual world through their own computer or they could be artificially intelligent computer processes. For example, a process could be left monitoring flight prices available from a travel agent. When a suitable price arrives, the procedure might inform the client or perhaps automatically procure the ticket.

It can be seen that distributed virtual reality can support trade and commerce and could easily make communal places redundant. It gives mankind the power it has always dreamed of. It allows an individual to be able to travel to anywhere and meet anyone in an instant.

The human race is outgrowing its planet at an alarming rate. If its materialism was aimed at virtual commodities they would never run out of space and resources. The only boundaries are those imposed by man's intelligence and imagination.

Any great change in civilisation comes up against criticism. Dispersing the population away from the metropolises does however offer many advantages. It can be argued that communicating through technology is antisocial. The truth is actually the inverse. Virtual environments could host almost any of the social activities seen today. There is nothing to stop people going to the theatre or even a discoteque in cyberspace. Distributed virtual reality pulls down the barriers of distance.

1.4   Applications

The previous section described what virtual reality can be used for. Many commercial applications have already been developed. This section introduces a number of examples and shows that the technology can be used for anything from rehabilitating the handicapped to monitoring the stock market or training pilots.

1.4.1   Rehabilitation of the handicapped

The technology of virtual reality deals in depth with natural interfaces between computers and man. This puts it in a strong position for overcoming any deficiencies in the input and output of either. For example, a person that can barely move their hand could wear a glove feeding their finger position into a computer which can then compensate for the lack of movement. One such system, developed by Greenleaf Medical Systems, substitutes keyboard input with gesture recognition [WALT92], and a manipulator control for mobility impaired people has been developed by the Swedish Institute of Computer Science [ANDE92]. Using the manipulator, a handicapped user can point to an object in a virtual world, a virtual robot then moves to that object and the user can operate a fine control to manipulate the gripper and pick up the object. This virtual modeller can be used to test the safety of a movement before it is enacted on a real robot.

Torlief Soderlund of The Swedish Handicap Institute, has cited four applications [SODE92] : sound oriented desktop for the blind, glove and gesture recognition, speech relearning for people with aphasia and exploring accessibility with wheelchair "input".

1.4.2   Training

Because virtual reality allows people to interact with things in a natural manner, it can be used to improve people's natural abilities. Jaron Lanier at VPL Research learnt to juggle four balls by juggling in virtual reality with progressive increases in gravity [SODE92].

Training for some skills can be expensive, impractical or even dangerous. Virtual reality can be used to do the bulk of an individual's training before they are ever put in the real situation, for example, British Airways now train their new pilots solely in simulators so that their first real flight of a passenger aircraft is a normal chartered flight. British Gas are looking into the possibility of using virtual reality to train operators of deep sea submarines used in the maintenance of oil rigs, whereby the submarine simulation improves the user's ability to navigate in dark water and steer the submarine in varying currents. This is made particularly easy because deep sea visibility is so poor that it can be adequately recreated by even fairly crude computer graphics.

Technicians required to fault find on complex systems will perform much more efficiently if they have had adequate 'hands-on' experience. However, large custom-built systems that are in constant use are not usually available for training purposes and unfortunately it is not cost effective to build extra systems that will only be used for training. Vega Space Systems Engineering are investigating the use of virtual reality in technician training systems. One such system developed by Vega, simulates faults on a complex rack-based computer system, whereby the user is presented with a view of the rack system as it appears in real life and they can move up to the rack and observe the state of warning lights. All the fault finding procedures, such as plugging in an oscilloscope or changing a card in the rack can be done within the computer model, fault finding on such a system could well become an addictive game with many technicians. A niche market therefore exists for virtual reality in training, the principle advantages being cost, portability, availability and configurability.

1.4.3   Concept design

Quality assurance being "one of the most important themes of software engineering" [JONE90], consists of verification and validation. The former is "building the product right" whereas the latter is "building the right product". Virtual reality offers the most realistic way of prototyping without the need to build a physical model. Verification is achieved through functional correctness checks, for example a user can test to see if they can reach the controls of a virtual car. Validation, that is testing the prototype against the requirements analysis, is particularly well supported in virtual reality, as a model can be represented in full size in a realistic environment.

A long term research and educational program has been established between Division Limited and the Computer Aided Industrial and Information Design (CAIID) group at Coventry University, the aim of which is to investigate the use of virtual reality in industrial concept design and evaluation. One application under investigation is concept car design, as shown in Figure 1.3, a goal of which is to demonstrate such cars by circling them around the user.

Figure 1.3   *Concept design of automobile*
Courtesy of Division Limited

1.4.4   Construction

The area surrounding the High Street of Edinburgh, called the "Royal Mile", has been modelled on a computer. Alan Bridges at the University of Strathclyde, has developed a virtual reality system used to test the visual impact of potential new buildings. Based around a Silicon Graphics 4D310 IRIS, the system offers good quality graphics at high speed.

The Department of Construction Management and Engineering at the University of Reading, under the Major Projects Co-ordinating Program, developed a computer aided building design (CABD) tool which

allows the creation and manipulation of solid models of building components. Further, Reading University's Cybernetics Virtual Reality
Research Group has created an immersive virtual reality viewer to allow
a user to "walk through" building designs developed on CABD.

One of the prime concerns in designing underground railway stations
is the potential spread of smoke in the event of a fire. Current computer-
based animation systems show a 2-D plan of the station and represents
expanding smoke clouds as flat grey blobs. This is adequate to show the
approximate extent of the smoke but gives very little impression of how
it would look like in real life. Research is currently being undertaken into
the use of virtual reality to improve visualisation. Using a head-mounted
display, a user could walk through a simulation of a smoke filled station
and actually observe the level of visibility.

1.4.5   Finance

Stock markets are not easy to visualise, although financial advisers often
have to make fast and important decisions having only a screen full of
numbers to guide them. Even more advanced systems such as bar charts
are inflexible and give little information. One of the major financial
institutions uses a desktop VR system to present a 3-D bar chart of the
market, in which prices of various commodities are shown with respect to
time giving a picture that looks like undulating hills. In cartesian terms,
the x, y and z axes represent commodity, price and time, respectively.

1.4.6   Molecular modelling

Molecular structures are three-dimensional and it is not intuitive to
model them using two-dimensional methods. Using immersive virtual
reality, a user can fly around a molecular model as big as a house and from
this they can build in their minds a much better picture of the structure,
as shown in Figure 1.4. By interacting with the model, a user can see the
effect of moving parts of the structure with respect to others. A consortium
has been set up between Glaxo Group Research, the University of York,
IBM (UK) and the VR manufacturers Division Limited, the initial aim of
the consortium being to investigate the use of virtual reality in molecular
visualisation, manipulation, interrogation of molecular structure and
menu-driven molecular model manipulation.

Figure 1.4   *Molecular modelling in immersive virtual reality*
Courtesy of Glaxo and Division Limited

1.4.7 Military

Military exercises are often large, extremely expensive and are also unpopular with local residents. With today's spy technology, there is a danger that much secret information about equipment and tactics could be gained by unwanted watchers, fortunately however, virtual reality offers a solution to all of these problems. SIMNET is a massive distributed tank battle simulator in the United States. In nine remote sites, 250 tank simulators each containing four crew members can rage virtual tank battles over hundreds of square miles. The simulation tilts and sways as the virtual tank moves across pot holes and through rivers.

The Royal School of Artillery at Larkhill in England have commissioned the development of a multi-user desktop VR system to train crews of ground-to-air missile launchers. Unlike SIMNET, this system is based around PCs linked over thin ethernet. The present system allows up to eight users to control missile launchers and attempt to shoot down enemy aircraft and the flying characteristics of the missiles are programmed into the software to give a realistic training experience.

Training people to shoot shoulder mounted missiles such as the "Stinger" is carried out at present in a large custom built dome in which computer generated images of targets are placed on the surface of the dome by moving projectors. TNO-FEL and Division Limited have teamed up to build an immersive virtual reality solution, whereby a user wearing a head-mounted display and holding a computer tracked metallic tube on their shoulder can turn and point the tube towards a target displayed in their helmet. The missile can then be launched and the user sees it travelling along its natural trajectory, hopefully towards the target.

1.4.8   Leisure

Virtual reality arcade games are already a common sight in large amusement arcades, in fact The Trocadero in London hosts three multi-user games. A VR flight simulator allows four people to fly biplanes and dog fight with an enemy led by the Red Baron, whereas a "run around and shoot" game allows four users to move around several chess board like plateaus connected by short staircases and shoot at each other.

The company who markets the majority of the arcade games, W-Industries, is expanding into the home VR market and is presently developing a low cost head-mounted display system including a compact tracking system.

Sega have stated a wish to put home VR systems in the shops before Christmas of 1993 with a system which will support a sub-$200 head-mounted display system. Sega have also publicly joined forces with W-Industries to produce an arcade game for 1994 [VRNE93].

1.4.9   Television

Cyberzone is a British Broadcasting Corporation television game show, shown in the UK, in which teams of two people try to overcome simple problems in a virtual environment. Cyberzone is non-immersive and displays the virtual world on a wall of large displays at the back of the set. Interaction devices such as tread mills and steering wheels add to the novelty. The show is aimed at the younger generation and is loosely based on the cult UK TV programme Red Dwarf. The setting is futuristic and reminiscent of the "Mad Max" films. The studio audience is a rowdy gang of "Cyberpunks" [GIBS84].

A more ambitious project cited by the UK television production company Broadsword, is a virtual reality take off of the inter European game show "It's a knock out" [CHIL93]. Theoretically, contestants could participate from studios within their own country all of which could be linked together over a high bandwidth communication channel. However, this project is only likely to succeed if a number of large corporations get together to fund it.

1.4.10 Art

Fine art is distributed in galleries all around the world and, although many books depict these works, they do not give any impression of the size or how they appear in real life. One of Turner's paintings in the London's Tate Gallery, has been designed with three perspectives in mind, in other words, there are three distinct vanishing points. This can only be appreciated by moving to the three perspectives, something that cannot be done with a book. Further statues and other artifacts cannot possibly be given justice in a two-dimensional picture.

A virtual art gallery loosely modelled on the Tate Gallery in London, has been produced by Philips Research Laboratories and in this a user, wearing a head-mounted display, is able to traverse three rooms taking in the splendour of texture mapped paintings. Tilting the head upwards brings the fresco into sight and walking through door ways brings the user into different rooms each dedicated to a separate Impressionist: Monet, Cezanne and Van Gogh. Impressionism, because it relies on bursts of colour rather than detail can be reproduced in less detail with limited effect on the appearance.

On a larger scale, a networked "virtual art museum" has been constructed at the Studio for Creative Inquiry at Carnegie Mellon University [LOEF93]. Contributors can link up to the network with anything from a simple modem and create their own exhibition. One project currently under construction is a "Visual Ancient Egypt" where a guide can direct groups of visitors around scale models of temples.

1.4.11 Aircraft Simulation

A conventional flight simulator is a physical model of an aeroplane cockpit incorporating a three-dimensional model, panoramic view and real time response. The typical cost for such a system is around £6,000,000 [VINC92]. Once built, any alterations are expensive, and such a simulator is large, heavy and extremely unportable. A comparable virtual reality flight simulator would probably cost under £1,000,000, would be very cheap to modify and could be transported in the back of a car. Once all the software objects required to produce a given virtual flight simulator have been produced, it is very cheap to develop simulations for other aircraft.

However, one argument often raised by traditionalists is that the trainee pilot cannot actually touch virtual buttons and switches. This can be overcome by using force feedback gloves which use piezo buzzers, needles or hydraulics to send tactile cues to the palm and fingers. Even if present virtual reality is not quite as good as a physical model, it could certainly be used for initial training.

1.4.12 Space

Moving in zero gravity is very different from walking on the ground, principally because the human brain has become used to the mathematics required to move the body and other objects under the effects of gravity and friction. In space where there is no gravity or friction, very different calculations have to be performed by the brain, for example, trying to move by firing a jet propulsion rocket can easily result in the astronaut going into a spin, another problem is coming to a halt. Further, an astronaut trying to push a heavy object might well result in the astronaut moving rather than the object. TNO Physics and Electronics Laboratory in the Netherlands are working with Division Limited to develop a virtual reality astronaut training system, as shown in Figure 1.5. This system will allow two people to train alongside each other in virtual space and carry out such tasks as constructing space equipment.

Figure 1.5   *Multi-user astronaut space-walk simulation*
Courtesy of Division Limited

1.5   Conclusion

Information is becoming ever more important in industry and commerce, however, the present methods of displaying this information are no longer adequate. Virtual reality can be thought of as the science of integrating man with information, and although it will be a long time before such things as virtual tele-conferencing come of age, in the meantime, virtual reality offers a good, cost effective solution for many engineering applications such as prototyping, simulation and system management.

Virtual reality is not just a "flash in the pan", it is one of the most widely applicable technologies since metal forging.

References

ADDI85   Addis, T., "Designing Knowledge Based Systems", Kogan Page, New Technology Modular Series, UK, 1985.

ANDE92   Andersson, M., "A virtual environment human/robot interface", 5th MultiG Workshop, Royal Institute of Technology, Sweden, 1992.

BENF93   Benford, S., "A distributed Architecture for large collaborative virtual environments", IEE Computer and Control Division Colloquim: Distributed VirtualReality, London, UK, 1993.

BENN   Bennit, J., "Lock Berkley and Hume", P95-96.

CARL93   Carlsson, C., "The Distributed Interactive Virtual Environments - architecture and applications", IEE Computer and Control Division Colloquim: Distributed Virtual Reality, London, UK, 1993.

CHIL93   Child, T., "Televirtual", IEE Computer and Control Division Colloquim: Distributed Virtual Reality, London, UK, 1993.

CVRRG   Cybernets Virtual Reality Research Group, University of Reading.

CYBE92   Cyberzone, BBC 2, Broadsword Television Production, 1992.

DIV93a   Application Brief, "Molecular Modelling", Division Limited, Bristol, UK, 1993.

DIV93b   Application Brief, "Training and Simulation", Division Limited, Bristol, UK, 1993.

FOSS93   Foss, J., Atkin, B. and Ackroyd, "Information Trading in Distributed Virtual Environments", IEE Computer and Control Division Colloquim: Distributed Virtual Reality, London, UK, 1993.

GEAK93 Geake, E., "Managers struggle to adapt to teleworking",
New Scientist, Volume 138, No 1876, ipc magazines, 1983.

GELE91 "Gelernter, D., "Mirror Worlds or the day software puts the
universe in a shoebox... How it will happen and what it will
mean", Oxford University Press, 1991.

GIBS   84 Gibson, W., "Neuromancer", Victor Gollancz Ltd, 1984.

GRIFF91 Griffin, M., "A Cynbernetic Perspective on Virtual Reality",
PhD thesis, Department of Cybernetics, University of Reading, UK, 1992.

HACK87 Hacker, P., "Appearance and Reality", P63, Bazil Blackwell,
1987.

HOFS79 Hofstadter, "Godel, Escher, Bach: An Eternel Golden Braid",
The Harvester Press Ltd, 1979.

HUME39 Hume, D., "Treaty of Human Nature", 1739, Book 1, P232-
233, Fontanna Addition, 1987.

JONE90 Jones, W., "Software Engineering", John Wiley and Sons,
U.S.A., 1990.

LOEF92 Loeffler, C., "Networked Virtual Reality", 5th MultiG Workshop, Royal Institute of Technology, Sweden, 1992.

MAJO93 Major, J., Conservative Party conference, 1993.

MOSH93 Moshell, J. and Dunn-Roberts, R. "Virtual Environments:
Research in North America", Virtual Reality an international directory of research projects, Meckler, ISBM 0-88736-
862-X, 1993.

QUIN60 Quine, W., "World and Object", MIT Press, 1960.

REA93   Rea, P. and S., Whalley, "Advanced Interface into network
management workstations", IEE Computer and Control
Division Colloquim: Distributed Virtual Reality, London,
UK, 1993.

ROBE92   Roberts, D. and Griffin, M., "Distributed virtual reality", Symposium: Virtual representations for design and manufacture, Coventry University, U.K., 1993.

SODE92   Soderlund, T., "Virtual Reality - Possibilities for the handicapped?", 5th MultiG Workshop, Royal Institute of Technology, Sweden, 1992.

SHER92   Sherman, B., "Virtual reality: a revenue generator for broadband?", Communications International, Volume 19, No 12, Periodical Publishers Association, 1992.

TNO93   Documentation 93/1803ST, TNO Physics and Electronics Laboritory, Netherlands orginization of applied scientific research, Netherlands, 1993.

SUTH65   Sutherland, I., "The Ultimate Display", Proceedings from IFIP Congeress, 506-508, 1965.

SUTH68   Sutherland, I, "A head-mounted three-dimentional display", proc Fall Joint Conf on Computers, 33, pp 757-764, 1968.

VINC92   Vince, J., "Waiting for VR", Symposium: Virtual representations for design and manufacture, Coventry University, U.K., 1993.

VRNE93   VR NEWS, Volume 2, Issue 6, Cydata Limited, July 1992.

WALT92   Walter J., "Datasuit and virtual reality: Advanced technology for people with disabilities", Technology and persons with disabilities, U.S.A., 1992.

YNGV92   Yngvesson, J., and Bengt, K., "Telepresence in conference applications", 5th MultiG Workshop, Royal Institute of Technology, Sweden, 1992.

Chapter 2

Interactive protein modelling

M. Hartshorn and E. Hubbard

2.1 Introduction

The past ten years has seen intense developments in the application of graphics and computing techniques and technologies in the study of the structure and function of proteins. This is a very demanding application. The complexity of a molecular structure is such as to be always pushing against the limitations of computing power or the speed of the graphics available. All of which is complicated by our naive understanding of the physical and chemical principles that govern molecular structure. As a result of these limitations, interactive molecular graphics have been crucial in the representation and dissection of structure, as many of the scientific insights have come only by exploiting properly the structural intuition of the scientist manipulating molecules through a computer screen.

Molecular graphics and modelling can be divided into two broad categories. In the first, there is a need to provide tools to build models that satisfy the restraints identified from experimental data. The second category includes a diverse set of methods that can be used to represent, interrogate and understand the chemical and physical properties and functions of molecular structures [ROBE86]. Some examples of these are given below.

2.1.1 Electron density fitting

The principle source of protein structures is X-ray crystallography. The result of these experiments is a three-dimensional grid of electron density values into which the atoms of the structure must be fitted manually by a crystallographer. Due to the size of protein molecules this can only be carried out on high performance graphics workstations. Current software [JONE78] allows the electron density map to be displayed as a series of perpendicular contour plots which resemble chicken wire (see Figure 2.1).

Various means are provided for positioning sets of atoms within the electron density. Interaction with the software is via a mouse and/or dial and button boxes. LCD stereo viewer glasses are used to provide a stereo picture. Electron density maps contain a large amount of information and it is usually necessary to draw them using vectors to allow for truly interactive graphics.

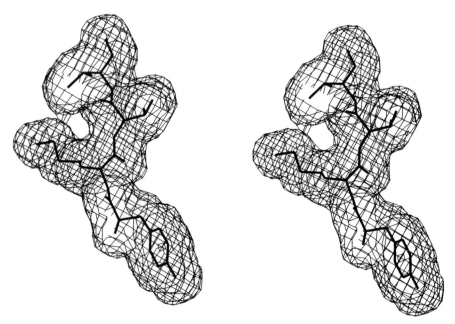

Figure 2.1   *Stereo diagram showing a small part of the electron density (thin lines) of a protein structure. The fitted protein structure is shown in thick lines.*

2.1.2   Structure and property visualisation

Once the structure of a protein has been determined the task of understanding how it works has only just begun. For this reason there is a large demand for software that allows the display of structures and their properties. For instance, one may wish to display the calculated electrostatic potential around a protein in order to find binding sites for drug molecules.

2.1.3   Structure interrogation

The current software used by molecular modellers these days also allows one to interrogate various aspects of molecular structures. Features include the ability to pick particular atoms in the structure and identify them or measure the geometry (distances, angles) of sets of atoms. Typical software also allows the superposition of several molecules onto a common set of atoms. This allows the scientist to inspect the similarities and differences between groups of molecules.

For a number of these areas, there are particular limitations in the currently available molecular modelling hardware and software. In particular, the visualisation and manipulation of molecular structures within a computer is difficult and unnatural. Even with the stereo implementations available using workstations it is difficult for a user to maintain the full three-dimensional perception of a structure that is important for visualisation, structural insight and modelling. Also the effectively two-dimensional interface provided by keyboard or workstation mouse is totally inadequate for intensive and natural manipulation of molecules against each other, or in trying to manoeuvre parts of a molecule to satisfy some experimental restraint.

As outlined above, interactive computer graphics has played an important role in the molecular modelling community over the past ten years. Software has been used for the construction of complex three-dimensional models of proteins, and stereo viewing devices have been found to be of enormous value in achieving this goal. As a result of this, it seemed timely to investigate the use of virtual reality technology, which extends computer graphics from the flat screen world of the monitor into three dimensions. The rest of this paper describes our initial research into the use of this emerging technology for useful molecular modelling and visualisation.

2.2   Pilot project

In collaboration with Glaxo Group Research, IBM (UK) and Division Ltd, we are completing a pilot project to explore the possibilities for virtual reality techniques in molecular modelling. This work was inspired by the pioneering work in this area by Fred Brooks and his team at UNC, Chapel Hill.

Virtual reality can offer two main advantages for molecular modelling. The first is in the area of visualisation. Molecular graphics systems have for many years incorporated stereo and real time motion to provide the necessary three dimensional perception of structure. In a virtual reality system, the user can wear a helmet containing two LCD displays.

The user is immersed in a molecular scene with full three dimensional perception and the molecule floats in front of you or can be around you. The second main difference of virtual reality systems is the provision of a natural interface between the user and the molecular scene. With appropriate interactive devices (such as hand-held 3D mice) it is possible to reach out, pick up and manipulate pieces of structure in a very natural way.

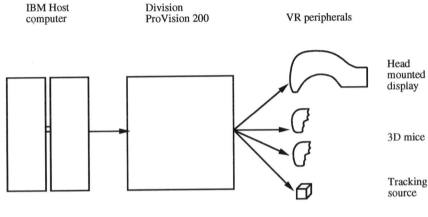

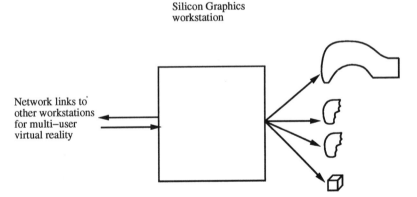

Figure 2.2   *Schematic diagram of equipment used for virtual reality molecular modelling.*
a)   Original equipment.
b)   Second generation based around conventional workstation.

The aim of our initial pilot project was to investigate the current state of the technology and whether it was appropriate for effective use in molecular graphics and modelling.

2.2.1   Equipment

The equipment used for this work was a ProVision 200 virtual reality computer manufactured by Division Ltd. (UK). This consists of a parallel architecture of Inmos transputers and three powerful Intel i860 processors. The transputers are responsible for communications. One i860 is used to render the virtual scene for each eye and the third runs the user's application program.

Images are displayed using a Virtual Research head mounted display. The head mount contains two LCD television screens mounted just in front of the left and right eyes. These are focused using appropriate optics. Stereo perception is created by providing the left and right eyes with slightly different views. By wearing a head set such as this the user feels 'immersed' in the scene. The tracking system used is a Polhemus Fastrak. The position of the head and two hand held 6D mice are tracked.

2.2.2   Results

The initial phase of this project has seen the development of a simple piece of software for molecular modelling and visualisation. The user is presented with a virtual molecular world in which their hands are represented as simple white arrows and the head and hands are tracked so the user can look around and touch objects present in the scene. Buttons on the mice are used for flying around in the virtual world and for picking objects. The software was developed using Division's proprietary virtual reality software dVS 0.1 [DVS]. The results to date can be summarised as follows:

Visualisation

We now have a reasonable grasp of the types of representation that can work in a virtual scene. The main constraint is resolution and the speed of the graphics. This combination means that reduced representations such as ribbons and cylinders work best for larger molecules. For smaller ones, ball and stick or Van Der Waals spheres can be used. The stereo perception is good, and you really do feel as if you are within the molecule. The scene is reasonably stable, and the system is not too tiring to use.

Manipulation and interrogation
This software first demonstrated to us the effectiveness of the 3D mice for manipulating molecular structures. If a user wishes to examine a particular piece of the structure then they simply pick up the object and turn it to the desired orientation, exactly as if it were a real, physical object. There is no need to think about rotating and translating the object around coordinate axes. In general, the resolution of the picking devices is adequate for most operations (you pick up what you think you should). One of the prototype applications we have put together is the two halves of a DNA helix separated in space. The challenge for the user is then to move them back into a double helix. This works very naturally – more so than on a conventional workstation. Our feeling is also that the spatial resolution of the mice should be adequate for interrogating individual atoms in a molecule.

General
The current generation of hardware is adequate for investigating how virtual reality can be valuable in molecular modelling operations. There are two obvious hardware limitations in the resolution of the head-mounted LCD displays, and the speed of the graphics. Building a real application will also require significant thought on how the user interacts with the system – there is no keyboard for command entry.

Unfortunately, it appears that most of the force-feedback devices, such as data gloves, are not yet reliable enough for our type of application. However, such developments would be particularly valuable, as in for example docking one molecule with another and feeling the binding energy and the bumps as the molecules overlap.

2.3   Further work

Having established that the technology is adequate to render and interact with molecules in a useful way, we are now beginning a more extensive project. In this we have started to use conventional Silicon Graphics workstations for the rendering, and these machines also drive the VR peripherals. The new system is illustrated schematically in Figure 2.2b. The software is based around the latest release of Division's virtual environment software dVS 2.0.

2.3.1   Results

This part of the project has seen the development of software with some chemical knowledge about the geometry of molecules and their interactions with each other. The software reads molecular models from a popular format of protein coordinate files. The molecules are visualised as sticks along the bonds between atoms. The default colours indicate the atom types.

Using a 3D mouse, different molecules within the scene can be moved around relative to one another. If atoms within different molecules come too close together these atoms are highlighted and the molecules will not be allowed to move any closer together.

It is also possible to change the geometry of the models by selecting a bond with the 3D mouse. When a bond is picked the direction of the users hand denotes which end of the bond is to be rotated. This is illustrated in Figure 2.3. If the bond is not part of a ring of atoms, then motion of the hand will cause the atoms attached to the bond to rotate around it. If parts of the molecule bump into one another they will be highlighted and further motion prevented.

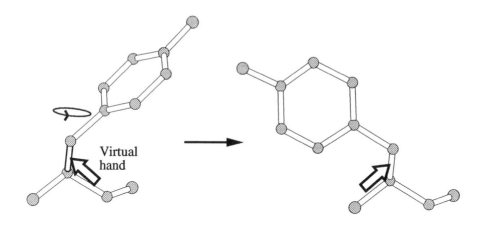

Before   After

Figure 2.3   *Changing the geometry of a molecule with a virtual hand. The user picks the highlighted bond. The hand is pointing towards the part of the structure with the ring of atoms, so this part is rotated.*

These simple extensions add tremendously to one's understanding of the structure and interactions of molecules. A simple example is the binding of the anti-cancer drug methotrexate (MTX) to the protein dihydrofolate reductase (DHFR). Simple examination of a line drawing of this protein—drug complex gives one very little idea why this compound binds so effectively to DHFR. However, by attempting to remove and then replace the MTX drug using this software, the user is made aware of the tremendous complimentarity of the shape of the drug and the protein binding site. With the use of such tools, a chemist may be able to design new drugs that may fit the binding site of DHFR better, and may lead to better chemotherapeutic agents.

2.4   Conclusions

Our experiences with virtual reality have been encouraging. The biggest advantage of such systems seems to be the ability to use hand tracked mice to interact with the molecular models. This allows for a very natural interface for many modelling activities.

The head mounted display provides very good stereo perception of molecular structure. However, there is a real need to improve the resolution of the head-mounted LCD displays, something which needs an advance in the underlying LCD technology. For our purposes, boom mounted displays or conventional stereo viewing systems may be more appropriate than head mounted displays.

In the future we aim to build some software systems which will allow some novel molecular modelling to be performed, exploiting the feeling of interaction between the chemist and the molecules. Although the technology is exciting and great fun to experiment with, our real interest is to provide scientific insight and modelling capabilities which are beyond the scope of conventional workstations.

References

ROBE86   Topics in Molecular Pharmacology (Volume 3). Molecular Graphicsand Drug Design. Editors A.S.V. Burgen, G.C.K. Roberts and M.S. Tute.Elsevier (1986).

JONE78   T. A. Jones. "A Graphics Model Building and Refinement System forMacromolecules", J. Appl. Cryst., 11, 268–272 (1978).

DVS   dVS. Software by Division Ltd., 19 Apex Court, Woodlands, Almondsbury, Bristol BS12 4JT, UK.

Chapter 3

Distributed parametric path planning

M. Griffin

3.1 Introduction

Virtual reality research is currently concentrating on the development of suitable hardware technology, the development of sufficiently powerful computing platforms and the design and implementation of the simulation and modelling elements. Recently, some thought has been given to the provision of facilities for the distribution of tasks and users over a network. A number of notable attempts have been made with regard to this, these are the Multiverse system, Dive II [FAHL92], and the commercial operating system DVS [GRIM93]. In each case an object oriented modelling approach has been adopted with message passing being implemented to change states within the model [THOM93].

These systems use broadcasting of events to inform all the tasks of what changes are currently being made to the system. This approach relies on fast transportation of these messages to keep all the modelling elements up to date. This is difficult to achieve in practice, particularly over wide area networks. The synchronisation and time delay problems encountered in this simple scheme may be removed somewhat if a time coded, parametric path planned approach is utilised. This approach will be explored in detail in the following pages.

3.2 Conventional virtual reality modellers

To fully understand the benefits of applying a parametric approach to virtual reality systems, current methodologies will first be discussed.

3.2.1 The shared model approach

Usually each computer taking part in the simulation has a complete copy of the virtual reality model being utilised by all systems on the network. For a diagram of this, please refer to Figure 3.1. This is necessary to keep network loading to a bare minimum, in that reading of the model can then be performed locally. As the reading of a database is by far the most common action performed (in rendering the graphics to the user and so forth), keeping this element close to the workstation makes a great deal of sense.

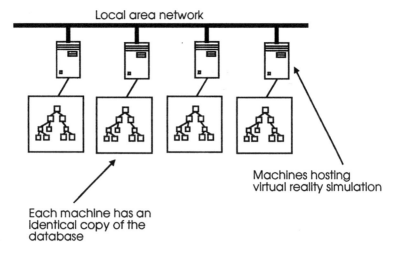

Figure 3.1 *The shared model approach*

Modifications of the database are generally far less common operations. These modifications may come from two sources: firstly applications packages running on the network and secondly users interacting with the model. When a change has been instigated on the model by one system, every system maintaining a copy of the virtual world needs to be informed of this. This is to maintain consistency as each system refers only to its local model. The change request is often handled in the form of a broadcast, in which the computer making the change sends a global message over the network to all the other machines informing them of the object that has been changed and the nature of the modification (see Figure 3.2). Other machines pick up this modification from the network and then update their local copies of the virtual world [ROBE92].

This approach works well as long as the systems in the network are connected together such that the network delays between systems are minimal in comparison with the overall cycle times of the simulation. In some synchronous systems such as VRT3, the trader machine has to physically halt until all the updates from the other systems have arrived before the next cycle time within the simulation may be attempted [ELLI93]. In a system with long network delays this would mean that the overall cycle time would be dominated by the network delay. In an asynchronous system, a long network delay may cause changes from outlying machines to force inconsistent and competing changes on the model. This is particularly a problem when considering two people attempting to co-operate over a large distance. Both of these effects are very undesirable [LEVI90] [COUL88].

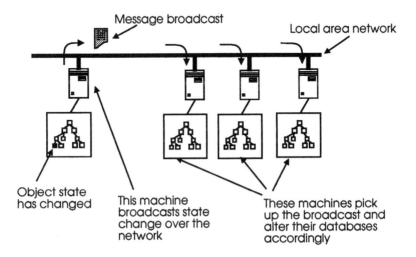

Figure 3.2 *A change request broadcast*

3.2.2 The discrete time approach

Many systems implement velocities and changes of state on a frame by frame basis. For instance, the path of a particle would be described as a position vector with an associated velocity to be applied to this vector on a frame by frame basis. In other words, between model updating times, the position vector is updated by adding the velocity component. This is then performed every time the model is updated. This simple approach thus permits the movement of objects within a virtual world. A modification of the iterative technique is used in many simulation systems in virtual reality.

Unfortunately, this simple approach is very dependent on the update time of the modeller running the simulation. If the time required to process the model varies (or any other element composing the overall system cycle time) then, with respect to real time, the path of the object will appear to speed up and slow down depending on system loading. As modellers will tend to run at different rates over the network, to ensure consistency in the modelling one system will have to be responsible for updating the position of the object and then broadcast the current modelled position of this object over the network.

The implication is that for a constantly moving object, the network will have to be subjected to a continuous broadcast of packets updating its position. In addition to this, the differing frame rates of the systems on the network will tend to cause severe temporal aliassing difficulties in its perceived position. For an example of this effect, please refer to Figure 3.3. Finally, with respect to systems at the end of a long communications delay, the position of the object will be lagging behind the modelled instance by at least the communications delay. These problems severely hamper the implementation of such schemes, unless the communications delay is insignificant and the frame rates can be guaranteed to be constant and synchronised. Over a wide area network, this is not feasible.

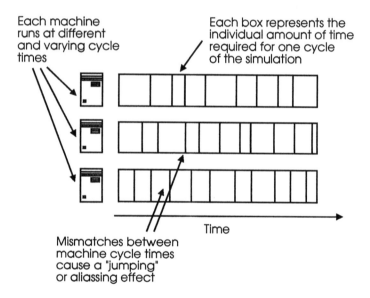

Figure 3.3 *The effect of different modeller frame rates*

In actual fact, even if the rendering time is constant, if there is an appreciable lag between calculating the model position and the display of that model, the model will always be temporally shifted. In most cases this is not a major problem, but if a real time simulation is being attempted, this fixed delay may be undesirable.

3.2.3 Collision detection

The subject of collision detection and other similar forms of object/object interaction will now be examined. As most systems use the discrete time approach, collision detection has to be performed on a frame by frame basis. This is very computationally expensive. The problem can be reduced by specifying the objects which are permitted to interact and by specifying bounding boxes and hierachies to limit the computational loading. However, fundamentally a check has to be performed in each frame time (see Figure 3.4). The complexity of the check will depend very much on the current level of object/object interaction. This is one potential source of varying system load and thus also of overall system cycle time.

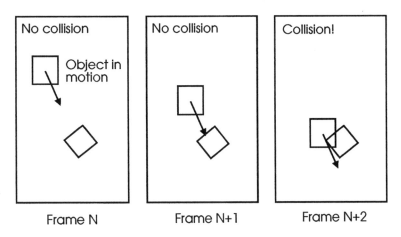

Figure 3.4 *Frame by frame collision evaluation*

3.2.4 User/Object interactions

For users interacting with the virtual world model, input from the body tracking systems at each user site is used to manipulate special 'user' objects. These objects then represent the user's body within the virtual world. Aside from the fact that the manipulating influence comes from a real person, these forms of interaction are indistinguishable from a semi random, discrete time source. The positions of the objects are updated after reading the user's body geometry in a cyclical manner. As with the object movement simulation, the new change in the user's state must be broadcast to the other systems over the network to keep their private models up to date. Each user on the network must perform this operation. If systems are running at different update rates, then the temporal aliassing noted previously with the discrete time method will occur and be potentially disorientating to a user.

3.2.5   General conclusions on current systems

All the elements listed above, including their faults and features, describe the most current approaches to distributed virtual reality operating systems. The main problems experienced are the effects of temporal aliassing and the susceptibility of such systems to delays in communications links.

3.3   The parametric path planning approach

It would be highly desirable if an approach could be found to remove or reduce the problems listed above [ROBE93]. One possible approach is the use of parametrically defined paths linked up to a synchronised clock system. This system will now be discussed, starting with the concept of the synchronised clock.

3.3.1   The concept of the synchronised clock

The parametric approach relies heavily on the existence of a global clock applied to all systems. This clock is effectively the real time clock of each distributed processing platform synchronised with some common time zone. To be reasonably effective, the synchronisation needs to be less than the level of the fastest update time across all systems on the network. In realistic terms this is only 1/50th of a second and is easy to achieve in practice. To counter clock drift and discrepancies in clock time on different computers, a clock server could be used. During slack periods on a local system, a synchronisation request may be made to the clock server. This is usually in the form of repeated requests, in which the network time of flight is measured. By compensating for this and by averaging the clock timings, sufficient accuracy may be obtained for even relatively remote clients to synchronise their local clocks. Please refer to Figure 3.5 for an example of this.

All interaction operations on model elements are time stamped with this clock standard. How this clock reference may be used will be discussed shortly.

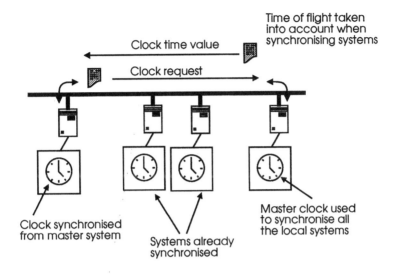

Figure 3.5 *The synchronised clock system*

3.3.2 *Parameterising of object paths*

In conjunction with the synchronised clock, all movements within the virtual world are encoded in a parametric form [SETH87], utilising time as the parameter. For the simple velocity case, in the new modeller the object would be defined as having an origin, a time code for when this origin applies a direction velocity vector and (in some cases) a termination condition (see Figure 3.6). The movement of an object would then be treated as a line equation, with the current position being calculated from the current value of the local system's real time clock and the vector information. Although this is more complicated than the simple iterative approach, it is always exactly correct for the current given time. For more complicated paths, higher order equations may be used, or a list of line solutions with appropriate time codes.

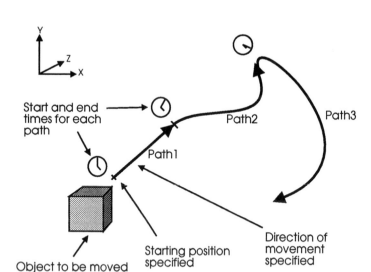

Figure 3.6 *Parametric path description*

3.3.3   Object path queues

If is possible to define a number of path elements for an object in advance. In a virtual world, as the whole scenario is defined beforehand, this can also include detailed path planning. For complicated paths, a queue approach may be used. Each path segment is defined in the manner listed above. By defining initial conditions, the path equation and suitable end conditions (including a terminating time code), the queue elements may each be consumed as the real time clock value surpasses the termination condition on the lowest queue element.

New path updates are entered into the queue in the following manner: Firstly the new path element is received. If the start time code on the new path is greater than the start code on the highest element, then the new element is added onto the queue and the termination time code on the previously top element set to the start time code of the new element. If, however, the start time code of the new element is less than the start time code of the highest element, then this element is removed, and any others, until the start time of the new path segment is greater than the element below. Then the element is substituted in as in Figure 3.7. Using this approach competing sources of path modification may write and overwrite future path planning and remain invisible to the users.

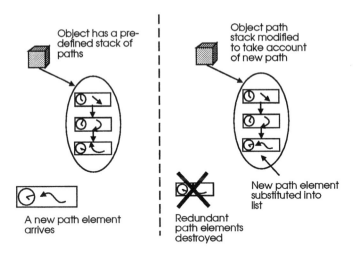

Figure 3.7 *Object path queues*

3.3.4   *Implementing a parametric shared model*

Implementing this new approach across a network is performed in a manner similar to the earlier systems. The model is still composed of objects with messages being passed between systems in the manner utilised by other systems. All objects now have a parametric path stack as well as their other attributes and the position and rotational elements of each model are now modified by commands placed on these stacks. As before, each computing platform in the shared model environment has a local copy of the virtual reality database. Changes to the database instigated by a system are broadcast to other members of the group such that their private models may be updated.

To re-emphasise, in the parametric system, all changes to the database have corresponding time codes associated with them and are stacked accordingly. Changes to an object's position and orientation may only be effected through the path queue. An object's path may be planned ahead through a number of path segments, each time coded to the absolute clock reference. New path elements broadcast over the network are intercepted and substituted into the stacks in the manner described earlier. In this way object/object interactions and user/object interactions may be captured and represented.

If we compare this with against the discrete time approach, as each system now has a complete description of the object path, both in its current state, and also some of the future states, then continuous positional broadcasting is unnecessary. This cuts down network traffic. Secondly as each system is now functioning independently, but is using a clock referenced parametric model, the position of an object may be calculated to be correct at the individual rendering times for each user. This means that motion will appear smooth and continuous, irrespective of frame-rates. Even if the loading of system varies and the frame rate drops, the real time position of the object will be accurate and the correct motion captured. Frame rate dependencies between individual sets of systems are also removed (e.g. PAL 50Hz and NTSC 60Hz).

3.3.5   Cache ahead collision detection

If the area of collision detection is examined, it may be seen that an approach different from the discrete time model may be utilised. As the motions of all objects are now defined in a parametric form, a collision detection operation may now consist of comparing sets of paths to see if they coincide with a certain tolerance (that of the individual object bounding boxes). If they do, a solution may be determined to see if they cross paths at the same instant in time. If this is the case, then a collision will occur. Fine grain collision detection may then be performed to calculate the exact effects on the two objects and compute the modified trajectories.

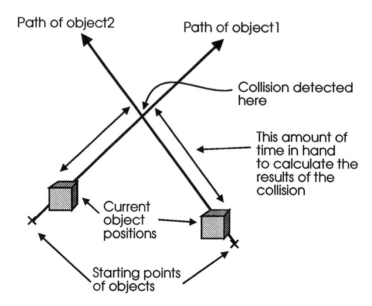

Figure 3.8 *Cache ahead collision detection*

Unlike the previous discrete time collision detection system, which only calculate on a frame by frame basis, this scheme can calculate collisions before they occur along the object movement path, thus removing these tests. As well as this, the approach permits collisions that are going to occur, to be calculated well in advance. This helps reduce peak computational loads on the processing platform. Please refer to Figure 3.8 for a diagram of this. Once the results of a collision have been calculated, computations may be applied to the new paths, such that the new resultant paths may be found a number of collisions into the future, processing power permitting. The need for a modifiable path stack system may thus be construed.

3.3.6   Fixed time overhead compensation

Current virtual reality systems perform modelling phases, communications phases and rendering phases. Unless the phases between the modelling interval and the final display of the result are insignificantly small, the picture presented to the user will always appear to be temporally shifted, as discussed earlier. The amount of temporal shift may vary with workstation loading. If an estimate of the amount of temporal shift can be made (by previous measurement), then the time code at which the model is calculated would be the current time of modelling added to an estimate of the temporal shift. This would ensure that the picture presented to the observer more strongly correlates with the real case of the picture actually displayed. In other words the temporal shift may be partially or completely eliminated.

3.3.7   The representation of user movement

Having examined the representation of object movement paths, particularly predefined ones, the subject of user/object interaction must be considered. Information about the user's movement is captured from the local tracking systems. This is then used to control a set of user objects within the local virtual world model, representing the user's body. At first sight, user movement might appear to be completely random in nature. This is not strictly true in that for reasonable intervals, joint movements tend to describe relatively smooth paths when in motion. At the start and end of movement the paths, naturally, become less well defined. In addition to this the initiation of a particular movement cannot be predicted.

User movement can therefore be converted to parametric form during the smooth movement stage, very successfully if sufficient bandwidth is available from the tracking system, by using curve fitting or Kalman filter approaches [FLET91] [WARW86]. This would then permit an estimate of the user's movement in advance and allow for the advantages of prediction stated earlier (see Figure 3.9). At the beginning and end of a movement phase, however, an accurate estimate is not possible and thus no path planning is possible.

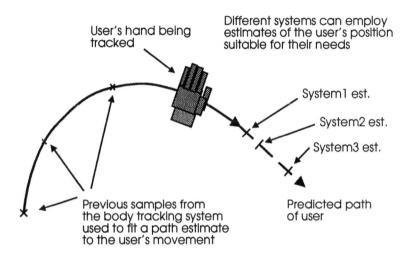

Figure 3.9 *Estimating the user's position*

Such a strategy for user movement may help to reduce the amount of network broadcasting required to update all the other virtual world models as to an individual user's movement. As most movements last less then 1/4 of a second the advantage conferred may be very small. This has yet to be determined. For the local systems receiving the user position broadcast, the level of temporal aliassing should be significantly reduced.

3.3.8   The effect of long communications delays

Having now considered the operational characteristics of machines local to one another, the effect of introducing large communications delays must be considered. In a standard system, the introduction of delay has significant deleterious effects on the level of perceived smoothness and system response. Both the quality of continuous movement and state transition behaviour are degraded by the added latency.

For the parametric system, if sufficient path planning has been obtained, then the models will maintain a very high degree of continuity from the user's perspective [GRIF91]. For changes made to the model by user/object interactions, then the latency will cause remote systems to initially "jump" to update to the new path plans, then to be in sync with the other systems. With suitably defined paths, the new path layouts should sufficiently similar to reduce the level of jumping.

If object/object interactions are considered, there are two possible answers. If the subject of changes brought about by collision type operations are considered, if these operations are all performed on each local workstation, to the same degree of accuracy, the model will be consistent across all workstations and the level of latency induced by the network will be nil. If the collision detection is not handled locally, then the latency problem will be as with the user/object interactions. If an applications package alters the database, the effect of this is identical to that brought about by user/object interactions. However, with an applications package there is considerable scope to design the package to minimise the level and type of path alterations in such a way to help reduce the level of object jumping.

3.3.9   Practical implementation details

The parametric path planning approach is currently being implemented in the current generation of virtual reality operating systems being developed at the Virtual Reality Research Group at Reading University. The LOKI II operating system, which will utilise this approach, is currently being designed for both PC and UNIX platforms, utilising TCP/IP and thin ethernet standards [COME91]. The system is being coded in C++ on both platform groups. A number of other university sites have agreed to assist in the testing and evaluation of the wide area network capabilities. Despite the fact that this operating system is being custom designed to implement the proposed scheme, it is felt that most current VR operating systems could be easily modified to take advantage of this approach.

The method, although conveying many advantages, does have some disadvantages. It is felt that the approach will require more processing power to implement than the discrete time method (for the movement aspect) but will undoubtedly save processing power when considering the overhead introduced by performing collision detection. This will require quite a sophisticated task scheduler to achieve the best performance over all regimes. This is currently being written. Any possible increases in processing required will still undoubtedly be swamped by that required for the visual and auditory rendering.

So far path planning of object position and orientation has been considered, but it is equally feasible to extend the technique to encompass other attributes of an object such that the system effectively becomes a parametric state planning system. In this way object shape, colour, texture, temperature, coefficient of restitution and other internal and external attributes may be modified and planned for in advance. If the object path stack is extended to include messaging capabilities and more complex behavioural elements, then the majority of the virtual world modelling may be performed in advance.

3.3.10 The general cache ahead methodology

The ability to do virtually all modelling in advance permits a general cache ahead methodology to be followed. In this scheme, the individual workstation platforms are always calculating at a flat out rate in an effort to predict the effects of the model before they occur. This calculation rate is increased in incidences of overall system slack and reduced in incidences of heavy computation load. In this manner of "feeding off the future" it is possible to borrow time usually used for modelling for something else (for instance graphical rendering) for short periods of time, as the calculations for the current time frame have already been computed. In this way, it is hoped that the overall graphical performance may be maintained at a high and even rate. This is very important for systems with potentially very variable loads.

3.4   General conclusions

In this chapter a new approach to the problem of sharing and maintaining models over a distributed virtual environment has been presented. This approach is deemed to give significant advantages over current approaches in the field of virtual reality. These advantages are listed below:

- The correct synchronisation of model movements over very large scale networks

- The ability to cope with large time delays inherent in wide area network systems

- The reduction of network traffic for modelling the movement/state change of objects in a virtual world

- The ability to produce visually correct models for varying frame rates

- The removal or reduction of temporal shifts

- The capability for increasing the level of smoothness when capturing user movement

- The ability to reduce the amount of processing required and level of peak loads when implementing collision detection

- The equalising of frame rates when implementing a full cache ahead system

The disadvantages that the proposed scheme imposes can be listed as the following:

- The need to redesign the operating systems to accommodate this scheme

- The increase of complexity within the operating system

- The increase in the amount of processing required for the movement modelling

- The need to set and maintain an accurate synchronised clock system

- The increased amount of memory needed per object that such a scheme imposes

- The confinement of having to define all object movement in a parametric form

The opinion of the author is that the advantages conferred in utilising such a system far outweigh the disadvantages. The implementation difficulties are not perceived as being insurmountable and it has been noted how such a scheme may be expanded to include the interfacing and control of telerobotic systems functioning over long telemetry links [GRIF92]. The system is being designed to include suitable connectivity for this field of operation.

References

COME91 Comer, D.E., "Interworking with TCP/IP", Prentice-Hall Publications, London, U.K, 1991

COUL88 Coulouris, G. F., Dollimore, J., "Distributed Systems - Concepts and Design", Addison Wesley Publishing Company, Wokingham, England, 1988.

ELLI93 Ellis, S., "VRT3 Reference Manual", Dimension International, Aldermaston, U.K., 1993.

FAHL92 Fahlen, L.E., Jaa-Aro, K.M., "Proceedings of the 5th MultiG Workshop", Royal Institute of Technology, Stockholm, 1992.

FLET91 Fletcher, M.J., "A Modular System for Video Based Motion Analysis", PhD Thesis, University of Reading, U.K., 1991.

GRIF91 Griffin, M.P., Mitchell, R.J., "The Use of Simulation Systems to Control Manually Operated Remote Manipulators with Long Pure Time Delays", Proceedings of Euriscom '91, Corfu, Greece, 1991.

GRIF92 Griffin, M.P., Bridgewater, C.E., "Presence II - A Testbed for Tele-Presence Experimentation, IEE Colloquium, London, U.K.,1992.

GRIM93 Grimsdale, C., "Distributed Architectures for Virtual Reality", IEE, Colloquium Digest No. 1993/121, London, U.K., 1993.

LEVI90 Levi, S.T., Agrawala, A., "Real Time System Design",McGraw Hill International, London, U.K., 1990.

ROBE92 Roberts, D.J., Griffin, M.P., "Distributed Virtual Reality Systems", SERC/DTI Symposium, Coventry School of Art, Coventry, U.K., 1992.

ROBE93 Roberts, D.J., Griffin, M.P., "LOKI II - An Archetecture for Distributed Virtual Reality", IEE, Colloquium Digest No. 1993/121, London, U.K., 1993.

SETH87 Sethi, I.K., Salari, V., Vemuri, S., "Feature Point Matching Using Temporal Smoothness in Velocity", Pattern Recognition Theory and Applications, NATO ASI Series, Vol. F30, Springer Verlag, Berlin, Germany, 1987.

THOM93 Thompson, J., "Virtual Reality - An International Directory of Research Projects", Meckler Publications, London, U.K, 1993.

WARW86   Warwick, K.,Rees, D.,"Recursive Methods in Identification",
Signal Processing for Control, Peter Pepegrinus Ltd, London, U.K., 1986.

Chapter 4

Virtual reality and rapid prototyping

I. Gibson, D. Brown, S. Cobb and R. Eastgate

Some of the proposed uses for virtual reality (VR) coincide with applications that rapid prototyping systems have been used for in the past. VR, with the ability to model real life environments, presents an ideal base for the design and development of new manufactured products. As a method of producing physical models directly from 3D CAD systems, rapid prototyping technology has also been used to prove and visualise new product designs. Here, an attempt is made to determine whether the two technologies are a means to the same end or whether they contribute towards a more efficient route to product development.

4.1 Rapid prototyping

Rapid prototyping technology is primarily aimed at reducing the lead times and costs associated with new product development. As a new product is introduced, or as old products are updated, various phases of aesthetic and functional design and testing take place. At some stage during this process, a physical model is required for evaluation. Using conventional processes and highly skilled artisans, the construction of this single model can take days, even weeks.

Rapid prototyping systems are capable of making highly accurate models, or prototypes, in a very short time. The starting point for such systems is a good quality 3D CAD system. Solid models are constructed using the CAD system and then post-processed in a layer format to make them suitable for the prototyping machines. Models made in this way are therefore limited only by the scope of the CAD system and the resolution and dimensions of the prototyping system. Models can therefore exhibit very complex geometries indeed.

As the understanding of rapid prototyping systems increases, so their applications will also increase. Jacobs [JACB92] describes five different uses for rapid prototyping systems:

1. Visualisation: It is always easier to understand an actual three-dimensional model than a drawing of it. The more complex the shape, the more necessary it is to fabricate it to understand its purpose.

2. Product verification: Once the product is defined, it is often necessary to determine its engineering properties and perform the function it was designed to achieve.

3. Iterative development: Product development is rarely 'right first time'. Using high speed fabrication, it is possible to correct mistakes early on, and at low cost.

4. Optimisation: Not only can design errors be rectified, but the choice of the best design can be made from an engineering point of view. Assessment of several acceptable designs can be made to achieve peak performance.

5. Fabrication or manufacture: This goes beyond the product development stage. Used with a secondary process, like investment casting, it is possible to go into small scale manufacture.

Jacobs classifies the process technology to make prototypes into four types:

1. Layer additive laser point-to-point fabrication
2. Layer additive nonlaser point-to-point fabrication
3. Layer subtractive laser fabrication
4. Layer additive nonlaser fabrication

The key word to their use is 'layer'. Parts are quantised in layers and constructed using a single repetitive process to build parts layer by layer. The general geometry of the parts to be designed is therefore unimportant.

The most common rapid prototyping system is undoubtedly Stereolithography (SLA), which is a system corresponding to type one. The idea of SLA is best illustrated by Figure 4.1. A laser is used to polymerise a liquid photomonomer resin. Wherever the laser falls, the resin solidifies (or cures) on the surface. It is therefore possible to solidify selective areas on a layer of resin. The support platform can then index down to allow the process to be repeated for further layers, producing a three-dimensional object (Figure 4.1).

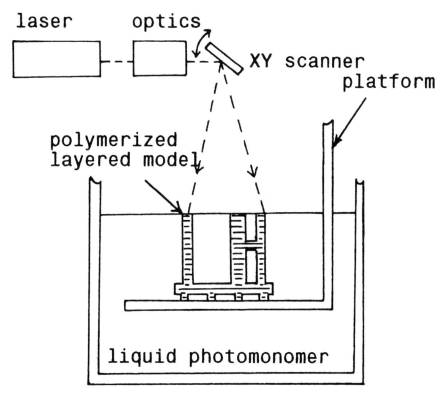

Figure 4.1   *Schematic diagram of operation of SLA machine*

At Nottingham, extensive research is being carried out on various aspects of rapid prototyping. The Rapid Prototyping Research Group has had the opportunity to see the development of this emerging technology as it has made its way across the Atlantic to the UK. The group has been able to log the development from only a few machines in 1990 through to the varied and dynamic industrial and research usage of today.

4.2   Virtual reality

Perhaps the best definition offered yet on the exact nature of VR comes from Zelter [ZELT92]. To qualify as a virtual reality interface system the virtual environment must offer a degree of three key components:

- Autonomy: objects must react to external stimuli, have collision boundaries and exhibit real world effects (e.g. coefficients of restitution, gravity and friction).

- Interaction: one must be able to manipulate the parameters of each object in real time.

- Presence: a crude measure of the fidelity of the viewing system.

Whether desktop or immersive, VR is computer modelling of real life as experienced through sight, sound and touch.

The above definitions suggest that designers and engineers who wish to address the problem of development and improvement of interactive design tools should consider how VR might benefit them. The Nottingham University Virtual Reality Applications Research Team, VIRART, was formed specifically to investigate problems of this nature. By building up an expertise in VR systems, VIRART aim to liaise with industry and identify where VR can be used. Current systems are not as easy to use and intuitive as they should be, and VIRART also set out to influence the development of the technology. With respect to industrial applications, VR appears to be useful in several areas:

- Where the real world is too inaccessible, too dangerous or too expensive to model in real life (e.g. nuclear installations)

- Where the worlds to be modelled are incomplete and require an iterative approach to determine their construction (e.g. control panel design)

- Where the ability to reorder the world requires the manipulation of parts in an unnatural manner (e.g. maintenance task training)

- Where some of the required attributes within the world are unreal (e.g. abstract modelling of management systems)

It is considered that when referring to product design, the use of VR relates mainly to the 2nd and 3rd of these points. Since Nottingham University has research groups working on both VR and rapid prototyping, it was considered appropriate to investigate where a combination of these technologies might lead. An experiment was devised to discover whether the use of one technology falls within the sphere of the other. In this case, it was considered that VR may only provide the same facility that a rapid prototyping system gives when used with an appropriate CAD system. This would then render VR redundant for product development. The emphasis of the experiment therefore changes slightly to a study of whether VR can provide more than CAD, thus relieving the comparatively expensive rapid prototyping systems of some of the product development burden.

4.3 Product development

Very important to this experiment was the interplay of aesthetic and functional design. Product designers are not always engineers. Designers may possess many technical skills, but they may not appreciate, and be conversant with, computer systems and software. Even if they can use CAD tools, the technical elements related to what is ostensibly an engineering environment may compromise their artistic ability. Similarly, functional products (e.g. engine components) may require other aspects of design to be considered. These considerations may not relate to the primary function of the product and the designer may therefore be unaware of their effect. For instance, the product may perform perfectly, but can the mounting points be reached for easy assembly and maintenance? Only when a part is put in context can it be seen whether it qualifies on all points. To this end, many products go through a physical modelling phase to prove the design fully.

To overcome the above points of conflict between flexibility in design against functionality in the most efficient manner, several solutions can be put forward:

- Use conventional modelling techniques in the first instance (such as clay and cardboard constructions), then digitise them into a CAD system. This provides a good compromise between free design and engineering design but is expensive and unlikely to be time efficient.

- Train aesthetic designers in CAD. Some designers are very proficient, and actually prefer using CAD software. Many are not however, and consider that such systems restrict their ability to freely design products. For functional products this is not so critical. Products with aesthetic properties (e.g. virtually all consumer products) require much consideration to the design media used.

- Form teams with both aesthetic and engineering designers in close consultation. This is perhaps the easiest and most common solution used in industry at present. However, inability to communicate between group members is also common, making this a potentially unstable situation subject to the characteristics of individuals.

- Improve CAD systems to reduce the skill requirement to operate them. This is the approach adopted by CAD companies. The solution in part is by providing software tools where it may be possible to perform the same function several ways. However, the CAD environment is always likely to exhibit an engineering bias even if VR based devices are used for the interface.

• Produce a form of 'digital clay' to allow modelling within a computer based system. This is the VR company approach. The interactive environment and tools for manipulation are there already. What is lacking is the ability to dimension the product effectively to allow for functional design.

It is obvious that the last two points are linked. CAD systems are being developed with VR based interaction. They are however significantly different from existing VR systems (the compromise being generally attributed to the perennial 'lack of processing power' problem). The panacea would be if VR systems could retain their excellent autonomotive and interactive properties, whilst adding advanced graphic definition and sculpture tools. The question therefore evolves into one of whether VR systems should be developed to look more like CAD systems? If they should then careful consideration must be given; not to what tools should be provided, but to what features of CAD should be left out to allow free expression in design. Since much is already known about CAD tools this experiment concentrated on whether it was possible to create a 'digital clay' approach using a VR system.

The VR companies are not unaware of the potential for their systems in a design environment. Grimsdale [GRIM93] states that 'there is a growing demand for advanced tools to shorten the design cycle, and enable companies to bring new ideas to market. For example imagine:

• A 3D sculpting system, which enables rapid conceptual design (e.g. shape modelling)

• An environment modeller, which allows you to place the design object in context, e.g. place the cam shaft in the cam guides; place the HiFi in a real living room; place the new desktop computer on a typical desk'.

This supports the various statements made earlier to justify the experiment.

4.4   Digital clay

The experiment took the form of devising some example worlds using the desktop VR system, Superscape. Any preference between desktop and immersive systems was not made at this stage. These example worlds were chosen to allow the design of specified products to take place.

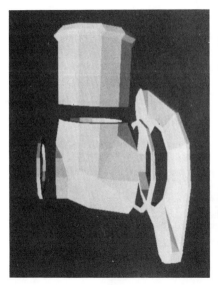 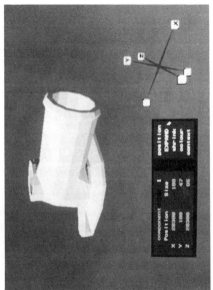

Figure 4.2 *Exploded view of*   **Figure 4.3** *Complete view of*
                thermostat housing   *thermostat*
                                                          housing

The first product chosen was a water thermostat housing for a small automobile. This product was based on a real design and is one that is very familiar to the Rapid Prototyping Group being the subject of many experiments in the past [DICK93]. This is primarily a functional product being a single mechanical structure, constructed from a few primitive component elements (Figure 4.2). As can be seen, the product looks representative but is far from accurate. The nozzle and base components can be distorted to provide a range of designs for assessment. If put in context with the rest of the engine, say, the product could be assessed for position and ease of maintenance (Figure 4.3). It is unlikely that anyone will be concerned about the aesthetic appearance of products like this one. As an example of assessment of suitability, a shorter nozzle could be functionally correct, using less material in its construction. It may however produce unacceptable difficulty when connecting the associated hose pipe. A larger nozzle, in contrast, may make it more difficult to access the mounting bolts.

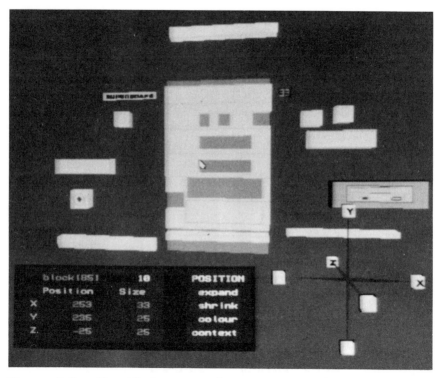

Figure 4.4   *Base design system for computer panel*

The second example world created was more detailed. This dealt with a product that combines aesthetic attributes with functional elements. The product chosen was the front panel of the 486 computer used to run the VR software. This panel is made up of sub-panels that form specialised elements such as buttons, disk drives and LEDs (Figure 4.4). These elements were combined with more general blank features that effectively fill in the gaps. These elements are initially laid out in front of a blank panel that represents the mounting conditions. The designer has the ability to place these components on the mounting panel. It is possible to change the size, shape, position and colour of each of these elements to assess the effects of different layouts.

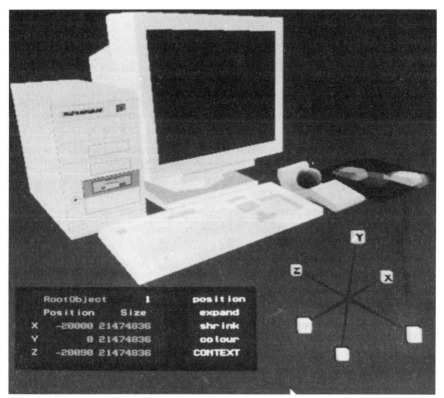

Figure 4.5   *Completed computer panel placed in context*

This computer panel is a consumer product and therefore must exhibit aesthetic as well as functional features. It is also part of a system that includes the screen, keyboard and mouse. It must therefore look pleasing within the context of the entire computer. Views must be acceptable from appropriate angles and each component can be positioned to achieve the best result in many scenarios (Figure 4.5). Assessment of ergonomic features like the clarity of layout and the position and size of control buttons can also be made for different configurations.

The concept of 'digital clay' is more refined in this second case. The elements can be distorted and positioned with ease by merely selecting an item using a mouse driven pointer. The world manipulation controls can then be used to control the attributes of each selected element. The disk drive has greater functionality than the other items and therefore its features are more constrained. Different elements can therefore be changed with different degrees of freedom, dependent on whether the context of their movement is appropriate.

4.5   Experimental analysis

It was found that the design environments were indeed easy to understand, use and manipulate. Rudimentary user trials showed that products could be rearranged with relative ease. Users also adapted to the environment with very little instruction, understanding both the reason for the experiment and the tools provided to change the world. Nobody, however, used the tools to produce products other than the ones designated; a point worth mentioning. These were however initial tests and further more detailed trials are essential to analyse fully its use as well as the necessary requirements for improvement.

The experiments have so far proved that new products can be designed using a VR based system. Both products were designed within a predefined context that did appear to limit the design scope. From the new designs created it was found that they were mainly assessed on aesthetic grounds for suitability. Both the constituent parts and the products themselves were found to be easily manipulated.

VR offers the ability to control software in a form that models real life. As in real life, the user performs a more qualitative assessment of the environment by way of comparison between objects in the working context. Quantitative tools were available in the example worlds in the form of readouts of component details. It was found that people using the worlds did not make use of these tools. The example worlds did appear to form the basis of a useful artistically biased tool for product development. It does not appear that quantitative elements are an essential requirement. What is essential is the ability to interface quickly and efficiently to appropriate CAD systems. These transported object descriptions can then be used by the design engineers and form the basis of an iterative process. Currently, Superscape supports the DXF file format but it is hoped that higher formats will soon be made available.

4.6   Future system developments

There are many features that currently do not exist that a designer would probably prefer in a VR based design tool. Some of these features relate to current limitations in the VR system used whilst others relate more to the example worlds created. The latter are obviously more easy to change under the control of VIRART. Some of these points are more for discussion than specified desired changes.

It is uncertain at this stage whether the example worlds should be context specific. It has already been stated that users did not attempt to design out of context. This may have been because all those who have used the system to date have had an engineering background. An aesthetic designer may have used the system differently but may also consider the example worlds too restrictive. The possible solution could be to present the system at two levels. At the low level is the purely creative environment with no predefined elements. Simple blobs of 'digital clay' can be combined to form more complex structures. At higher levels, objects appropriate to the design context will be provided alongside these simpler elements. The next test will be to provide designers with non-context driven tools to see whether they can be used to generate something completely original.

The speed of response and resolution of the system are both inferior to what would ultimately be required. This does not mean however that true, life-like representations are essential to the working of the system in this context. As the number of facets increases on the screen the speed of response does appear sluggish on what is a comparatively slow machine (PC 486 running at 33MHz). As such for simple objects the speed is probably adequate making it useable in its present form.

So far the examples have not allowed the user to define custom elements. A facility to create new shapes with different shapes, surface features, textures, texts etc. is desirable. This could constitute a form of digital pen and paper to be used along with the digital clay modelling system. In effect, this becomes CAD meets DTP in 3D.

Continuing on from this point, it is also not possible to manipulate parts as much as would be desired. For example, at present the disk drive cannot be turned on its side. This stands to highlight one of the main differences between desktop and immersive systems. The manipulative ability within an immersive system appears to be more intuitive than a desktop system through its ability to provide more direct contact with the virtual world. With the desktop system, parts are manipulated via the world control tools rather than directly. With an immersive system, the tendency would be to literally grab hold of the object. Desktop systems are attempting to overcome this problem by integrating with 'data glove' input devices. It remains to be seen whether this will be successful.

Finally, no consideration has so far been given to animation within the worlds. Most designs tend to be static in the first instance but interaction between associated moving parts is often very important in later stages. These are features inherent to VR systems and it is expected that further developments will incorporate animation.

4.7 What about rapid prototyping?

When the stage is reached where quantitative test data is required then physical prototyping becomes necessary. Rapid prototyping systems shorten this process dramatically making it possible to recoup a significant capital investment in a short period. The operation time of these machines is still significantly long. Generally parts are in a finished, useable state in around 2 days. If all that the part is required for is to assess factors like dimensional fit, accessibility, optimal position, aesthetics, then a system that operates in real time is much more appropriate.

The primary use for rapid prototyping systems is not therefore in the qualitative assessment phase of product development. Manufacturers are realising this and much more use is being made of soft tooling processes (like investment casting) to produce test parts and for short production runs. This is a much more important role for this technology to fill. Competitive marketing policies still dictate that physical models are created for purposes like tendering and user evaluation. VR, with its capacity to model real life, provides a practical replacement for rapid prototyping in this sense. VR fulfils at least some part of the first four uses for rapid prototyping mentioned by Jacobs earlier. There is no possibility of VR fulfilling the fifth use. With VR supporting, the more expensive rapid prototyping technology can therefore be considered free to perform the more production related tasks.

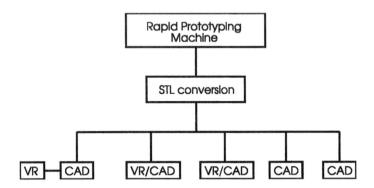

Figure 4.6   *Proposed configuration for optimum use of rapid prototyping system*

The ideal product development environment is therefore a rapid prototyping base supported by CAD systems to supply the engineering detail. VR systems will be linked to the CAD systems that are designated for product development with aesthetic content. A possible layout can be seen in Figure 4.6. This Figure also shows the post-processing unit for conversion of CAD solid models into a layer format suitable for the rapid prototyping machine. The ratio of machines is indeterminate but one rapid prototyping machine could quite easily support four or five CAD workstations with perhaps two of these working along with VR software (preferably on the same platform). This ratio of CAD to rapid prototyping machine is likely to be larger where VR is employed.

In conclusion, VR is cheaper, faster and less technical than rapid prototyping. VR provides a complimentary technology to rapid prototyping, but the interface is most suitably accommodated through CAD. The use of VR makes some of the intended uses of rapid prototyping redundant, but it is impossible to use VR beyond the point where testing or production is required. After all, it is only software.

References

JACO92   Jacobs P., "Rapid Prototyping & Manufacturing", pub. by the Society of Manufacturing Engineers, USA, 1992, ISBN 0-87263-425-6.

ZELT92   Zelter D., "Autonomy, Interaction and Presence", Presence, Vol.1, no.1, 1992.

GRIM93   Grimsdale C., "Virtual Reality: Evolution or Revolution", Proc. 3rd conf, Virtual Reality International 93, VR 93, Olympia, London, April 1993.

DICK93   Dickens P.M., Cobb R., Gibson I. and Pridham M.S., 'Rapid Prototyping using 3D Welding', Journal of Design and Manufacturing, Vol.3, no.1, March 1993, pp39-44.

Chapter 5

Computer-aided building design and construction

C. Bridgewater

This chapter explores some of the potential applications of virtual reality to computer-aided building design and computer-integrated construction. Particular emphasis will be placed on the use of modular forms of construction which are suitable for automated design and erection techniques. Previous systems in the field will be described and potential areas of investigation will be explored with reference to the peculiar needs and requirements of the construction sector.

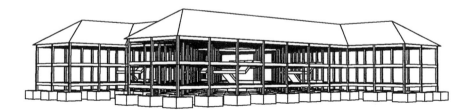

5.1   Introduction

The popular image of the construction industry in the United Kingdom is one of an unsophisticated dinosaur which continually fights against changes to its archaic attitudes and working practices. Despite this negative image, however, computers have been used in the construction industry for many years. Their use was initially for word processing and accounting, but more recently computers have been used for draughting and for structural design. It is true to say that the industry has been cautious in its attitudes towards computerisation, which has also been reflected in its approach towards automation and prefabrication. The industry is notoriously conservative and always seeks to use technology which is firmly established. It is only now beginning to harness new technology, primarily because of a deep-rooted and long-term lack of investment. As has already been pointed out by an American researcher:

> *...the most important underlying concerns of this*
> *industry are the problems that construction has been*
> *trying to cope with for more than the last decade,*
> *namely decreasing productivity and increasing costs.*
> *Progress in construction productivity as well as*
> *progress in productivity in other industries is a*
> *progress stimulated by work experience, the*
> *development of management techniques, by the desire*
> *for better products and improved overall economic*
> *efficiency, but mainly by the development of various*
> *relevant branches of science and technology. This*
> *indicates a need for continuous effort to utilize such*
> *new scientific and technological achievements in*
> *increasing the effectiveness of the construction process*

[SKIB 1988]

Given the preceding comments about the attitudes of the construction industry towards new technology, it should come as no surprise that the use of virtual reality in construction is almost unknown. There are, however, many areas where the industry could benefit from the improved human-computer interfaces that VR technology promises. If anything, it is the drive towards improved productivity that will eventually lead the industry away from the idea that VR is anything more than a marketing gimmick or a sophisticated toy.

The construction industry currently uses computers to automate simple manual tasks such as draughting and certain aspects of engineering design. Most of the commercial draughting packages began by replacing a drawing board with a cathode-ray tube. Most of these packages can exchange drawing data on a fairly rudimentary level, but international standards based around product model data have not yet been forthcoming. The ISO standard called IGES was an attempt to rectify this, but was unsuccessful in displacing AutoCAD's proprietary DXF standard.

More recently, applications have been marketed which allow data relating to numbers of components on the screen, areas of walls and so on, to be gathered. This information can be passed to a commercial database for later processing. Some consultants offer CAD data exchange services and others require contractors and sub-contractors to use CAD systems which can handle specified formats. Electronic data interchange of this kind is still in its infancy in the construction industry even though it is being strongly promoted by leading construction companies [BRAD91].

Commercial analysis packages are generally based on matrix methods for solving full or partial stiffness equations. Some packages include integrated design and code-checking modules. Post processors analyse the members and make assessments of size and shape based on codes of practice and statutory rules [FUKU88, STON86]. It is not a great leap to feed this information back to a CADCAM system which then orders the necessary materials and instructs CNC tools to cut and finish the components [OLIV90, RETI89, YAMA90].

Services engineers use computers to model the effects of solar gains on heating and the requirements for lighting within a building [FAZI89ab]. Meanwhile, some of the more enlightened architectural practices realised the potential of computer graphics as a marketing tool for their designs and have developed considerable expertise in the visualisation of their building models. Solid modelling and photo-realistic rendering are popular with architects and developers [COOM89abc]. The latest computer graphics techniques are used to make the CAD models appear as lifelike as possible to a potential client. Taking this approach further, urban planners and designers have made detailed CAD models of huge city areas in order to assess the impacts of proposed developments [MITC77].

Traditional office skills such as typing and book-keeping are becoming computer-based, so that word-processors and spreadsheets are now commonplace [CSSC89]. Similarly, stock control and invoicing are becoming computerised, so that the information infrastructure of a large construction company can rival that of any manufacturing organisation. What is not happening is the integration of these disparate and wholly separate sub-systems into a unified whole [FINN88]. That is, the automation is piece-meal and is not likely to yield all the benefits that it might otherwise be expected to bring [PAEK90].

What is currently lacking is a computer infrastructure that incorporates all of the systems described above and more [ATKI89]. Such an infrastructure would encompass all aspects of a company's business, linking component manufacture to payroll, site-based staff to office automation and so on. Clients would be able to communicate electronically with the company: not merely by use of a facsimile machine, but by direct interaction with the company's own information systems. The data that would be available to the directors and managers would be recent and relevant. Such is the future of information technology in the construction industry, if the companies choose to go down that route [ELMS72, CSSC90].

Potential application areas for VR systems in construction encompass all of the areas mentioned above. However, some of the problems that need to be overcome before the technology is used more widely include the strain associated with even short times in contemporary immersive systems, data interchange standards, limited scope for interaction with the environment, and the computational problems associated with modelling real-world physics. The major hurdle faced by researchers and developers of systems will be that of acceptance by a conservative and apparently technophobic industry [BROW89].

5.2   Background research

There is currently some debate in construction circles as to what actually constitutes a VR system. Some proponents of head-mounted displays contend that a system can only be deemed to be a true "VR" system if it uses the HMD as its primary output to the user. A logical extension of this view is that a VR system needs to incorporate other sense stimuli such as binaural or stereo sound, odours, tastes and touch stimuli as well as the HMD. The ultimate goal of such a view seems to be the insulation of the user from the real world by abstraction layers of their own choosing.

An opposing viewpoint contends that the preoccupation with display technology is missing the point. Rather, it is the generation and manipulation of a computer model of the real world that is the important characteristic of a VR system, not the manner in which the model is presented to the user. To take this latter view to an extreme, a simple scheduling package might be considered to be a VR system if it models some aspect of the manufacturing and delivery process that the site staff need to deal with.

In many respects, the debate between "immersive" and "non-immersive" VR systems mirrors that which took place when expert systems became popular. The arguments about what constituted "expert performance in a given domain" obscured the fact that the new methods of programming and techniques for eliciting knowledge produced useful computer systems. What is not widely appreciated is that object-oriented programming methods sprang directly from research into expert systems.

A similar example relates to the advent of design for automation in the manufacturing industry. It was obvious that assemblies would have to be re-designed in order to suit the characteristics of robots vis-a-vis people. However, it was noted that in many cases, the robot-friendly designs were also easier for people to assemble. In extreme cases, this led to the dropping of the capital-intensive production machinery in favour of the human workforce [BROW88]. It is interesting to speculate as to whether the introduction of VR interfaces to existing packages will lead to a more rational use of computers in the construction industry.

In order to understand how VR might impact the construction industry, it is necessary to present some of the fundamental concepts of this recently emerged technology. Therefore, this section will present some of the early examples of research into virtual reality as they exhibit the ideas more clearly than some of the later ones. Likewise, some of the earlier systems developed for computer-aided building design will be used to illustrate the essential features of the VR-based building design system. It will become clear from the discussions that follow that construction is a natural area for the application of VR and tele-presence systems because of the visual nature of much of what is done.

5.2.1 Previous research in virtual reality

Two examples of early VR systems are the head-mounted display developed at the University of Utah, and the three-dimensional computer graphics workstation developed at Loughborough University of Technology.

The Utah VR system consisted of a helmet assembly which was attached to some fixed point by a series of mechanical linkages. By measuring the relative motion of the linkages, it was possible to derive estimates of position and orientation of the helmet. A similar method was used to derive the position and orientation of a hand-held device which allowed the user of the system to interact with the computer-generated model. This 'wand' could also be used to draw crude 3D forms or to edit the model. The world model was held by a mainframe computer which generated a stereo pair of images using the position and orientation of the head of the user. These were fed to a pair of displays on the helmet via suitably arranged optics [SUTH68].

The Utah system demonstrated that it was possible to track the head and hand motions of a user and to generate scenes from a model database which were consistent with that motion. While it was crude in its construction, the system exhibited many of the features that have been incorporated in modern VR systems such as that marketed by Division in the UK. However, the computer technology of the mid-1960s could not support models more complex than wireframes and ran very slowly even at this low level of detail. The apparatus was very heavy and cumbersome to use, which caused undue strain to the users.

More recently, researchers at Loughborough implemented a more practical VR system by using ultrasonic range finding to determine the position and orientation of the helmet. This meant that the helmet was much lighter than had been possible in the Utah system. Another departure was the use of a pair of motorised flaps to mask one eye alternately. Computer images were generated according to which eye was 'open' at any given time. In this way, it was possible to generate a crude stereo pair using a single display. More modern systems use a pair of glasses with lenses covered with an electro-sensitive liquid crystal coating. Such coatings are opaque when a current is passed through them, but rapidly clear again when the current is switched off.

The images that were generated were wireframes, but the system as a whole was considerably easier on the users as there were no mechanical linkages to cause fatigue. More recent versions of this system are considerably more sophisticated, incorporating solid-fill graphics and much larger databases of objects. They have been successfully marketed as arcade games by a company started by one of the original researchers from Loughborough.

5.2.2   Previous research in computer-aided design

In the late 1960s, attempts were made to model components of contemporary building systems and to automate the design and evaluation of projects. Development continued throughout the 1970s and culminated in systems such as OXSYS, TechCrete, and SHSS [HOSK72, MYER75, BIJL72]. The main features of these systems were that they took a design from a conceptual sketch, through the process of assigning components and on into the production of working drawings. They invariably finished by making lists of components which could be ordered and then erected on site [DIST72]. The emphasis of researchers, however, was on the evaluation of alternatives, rather than the automation of design tasks [BIJL79].

Unfortunately, the computer technology of the day could not cope with the storage requirements of the building models which were created [ARC73]. Also, the computer packages were tied too closely to individual building systems, which caused problems when the building system was discontinued [EAST72]. A notable exception to this was OXSYS which was evolved into a successful commercial CAD system by McDonnell Douglas Information Systems.

OXSYS was developed to aid in the design of hospitals using the Oxford method for hospital construction. The method used a narrowly defined component-based building system, and was adopted by the Oxford Regional Health Authority in the late 1960s. Component locations were given using a basic command-line interpreter and the joint details were taken from libraries of data derived from past projects. Plans and elevations were developed from data held in OXSYS and an erection sequence could be devised. Lists of components and their approximate costs were also produced. It was planned to add daylight simulations and energy assessments of the plans, but these were never fully implemented [RICH76].

Researchers at the Departments of Architecture and Civil Engineering of Carnegie-Mellon University developed an integrated software environment which catered for the design of multi-storey framed buildings. The description of the building model held by IBDE was not necessarily a 3D volumetric one because IBDE is not a component-based system. Much of the complex structure in IBDE can be explained by this fundamental point [ADEL88]. A detailed history of the design process was kept, so that the system would later be able to answer queries about its reasoning.

Because of the way the data manager presented the building model to each software module, each of them saw only certain attributes: none of the packages saw all of the slots, because none of them needed to [FLEM88]. These restricted views of the building model were communicated by ASCII files which were then read in and processed by the module. All output was similarly directed to ASCII files which the blackboard then processed on behalf of the data manager. The control hierarchy was intended to be generic and to have as little domain knowledge as possible built into it [ZOZA89]. All input and output to the user was conducted via graphical displays and menu structures.

Following on from the earlier HI-RISE system, IBDE was a useful testbed for investigating the implementation issues associated with general-purpose computer-aided building design tools. Because it was not bound up with a component-oriented approach to construction, it had to be more complex than other systems such as OXSYS. It successfully demonstrated that a distributed model of building design and scheduling could be supported by currently available computer technology. Its use of the blackboard system and dedicated data translators for software modules points the way to a powerful method of describing buildings correspondingly for each member of a human design team [MAYA88].

5.2.3 *Examples of tele-operated construction plant*

Tele-operation is where an operator uses a piece of machinery at a remote location without being in direct physical contact with the device or its load. Examples abound of systems which use radio control to drive robots or other devices, such as the concrete finishing robot marketed by Shimizu Corporation of Japan. Other systems incorporate force feedback to give the operator a sense of how much effort the robot is having to apply. When used in conjunction with a VR interface, tele-operated vehicles give their user the impression that they are in the environment alongside (or in place of) the robot. Situations where this applies give rise to what are called 'tele-presence' systems.

Some interesting enhancements of existing construction plant equipment has come through the addition of sensors and on-board computing. At the same time, there have been studies of the ways in which experienced personnel use plant and equipment [SEWA88]. The results of these studies have enabled the development of strategic control mechanisms and operational strategies for existing plant and equipment [BERN89].

A tele-operated excavator has been constructed using simple vision systems, binary switches and proportional controls which are remote from the vehicle cab [WOHL89]. The machine can then operate safely in hazardous areas, with the driver well away from the vehicle. Likewise, the US Air Force have modified several of their excavators to have a tool-changing capability and have equipped them with suitable controls so that they can be operated remotely. In order to allow an operator to use the back-hoe arm as an extension of his own body, a control system was designed by considering the ability of a typical excavator to apply a force over its operating envelope.

An ergonomic manual control system was designed for a large hydraulic crane carrying a robot attached to its remote end [ALCI89]. One joystick controls the crane, another controls the manipulator. The ergonomic system as a whole can either be used to control the manipulator directly or can be integrated into a computer graphics simulator. This is used to test the system and/or train operators. The principal use of the crane is to insert large diameter steel pipes into racks as part of the erection process for chemical plants.

5.2.4   The LOKI-MPCP interface

This section describes work that was conducted jointly by researchers in the Departments of Cybernetics and Construction Management & Engineering at the University of Reading. An existing computer-aided building design system was modified to allow its results to be visualised using what was then a prototype VR system.

5.2.4.1 The Reading virtual reality workstation

The prototype VR workstation developed at the University of Reading was based around a Commodore Amiga computer delivering stereo image pairs to a helmet-mounted display. Binaural sound was also supplied to the user via a pair of speakers attached to the helmet. Two liquid crystal displays with resolutions of 200 x 300 pixels were attached to the computer and the output from them was sent to an optical system which allocated one display to each eye. The general arrangement of the VR workstation is shown in Figure 5.1.

Figure 5.1 *Overview of VR workstation*

The two displays were synchronised by splitting a single RGB output on the Amiga into red and green components. One of these signals was sent to each eye via a modulator which also ensured that the colours on each screen were ultimately consistent. The end result was a stick or wireframe image of the scene which the operator was able to interpret as a 3D image. The orientation and position of the user's head was tracked using a magnetic tracking system which used three mutually-orthogonal coils. The approximate working volume of the tracking system was a cube with sides of two square metres.

An object-based workserver was developed for this project which has been detailed elsewhere [GRIF92]. The main features of the server software were mechanisms for supporting an object-oriented model which could be hierarchically structured. Slave programs could be attached to objects in the hierarchy which allowed the objects described to have independent motions and properties. Artificial worlds could be constructed by various applications packages or by generating a unique program structure using a script language developed specifically for this system.

One extension of the system was to incorporate data sources other than the computer and to overlay the results of some computer analysis onto the real world images. To illustrate this, a pair of cameras and microphones were attached to a PUMA 560 robot and used to drive the robot in a workspace which was remote from the VR workstation. Synthetic images were generated by the computer and combined with those from the robot. In this way, it was possible to add information about the environment which would not otherwise have been available to the user. The principal elements of the tele-presence system are shown in Figure 5.2.

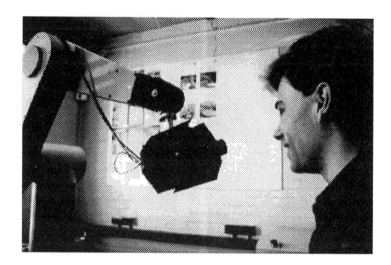

Figure 5.2 *Elements of tele-presence system*

5.2.4.2 Master Project Co-ordinating Program

The Master Project Co-ordinating Program (MPCP) was devised to explore the technologies required for computer-integrated construction. In design theory, it has become axiomatic that much useful information is discarded as paper drawings pass between the designers, the manufacturers and the constructors [SMIT89]. If the constructors had access to the same view of the building that the designers had and were able to influence the course of the design from an early stage, then it seems plausible to suggest that site operations would progress much more smoothly. It was decided to focus on the construction of highly-serviced structures found on business parks. Such buildings are generally either two or three floors in height and are simple layouts on plan [BRID89].

A modular, industrialised building system was developed which took advantage of manufacturing automation and on-site robotics [BRID90a,

IBAN90]. At the same time, a general building model was developed using a hierarchical structure of 3D entities. These were implemented using solid modelling techniques and an object-oriented representation scheme [BRID90b]. A blackboard shell was used to develop a supporting kernel for the model which acted as a filter to the design changes that were requested by the designers [BRID93]. The general architecture for the MPCP is shown in Figure 5.3.

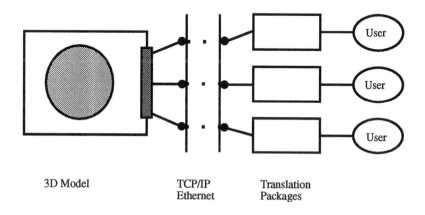

| 3D Model | TCP/IP | Translation |
| | Ethernet | Packages |

Figure 5.3 *General architecture of MPCP design system*

Some of the results from the building design system are shown in Figure 5.4, where a volumetric description of the building housing the School of Engineering & Information Sciences at Reading University is turned into a structural frame and external cladding using the components in the building system. Alternatives can be generated quickly and evaluated using cost, aesthetic or other criteria [BRID92].

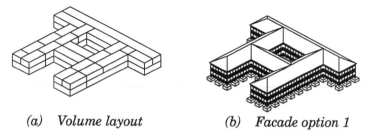

    (a) Volume layout   *(b) Facade option 1*

Figure 5.4 *Views of the finished school building*

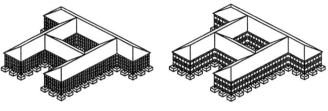

(c)   *Facade option 2*   (d)   *Facade option 3*

Translation packages were written to transform the building model into a representation that was suited to the needs and requirements of individuals within the design team. Their decisions were then translated back into a form that could be incorporated into the building model before the next round of design could continue. This meant that the design process was essentially serial in nature in that only one designer could work at a time using the latest state of the building model. The results of any design changes would, however, become immediately apparent to all of the other designers who would then be in a position to compete for the attention of the design system.

The Reading VR workstation was attached to the existing MPCP infrastructure by writing another translation package to turn its 3D model into a LOKI-readable form. Once this had been read into the workserver software, it was possible to wander through the LOKI-maintained model of the building. In the demonstration system, it was not possible to interact with the model by changing the locations of the columns or beams. However, in principle there is no reason why this should not be possible in the future. Sample output from the VR system is shown on the following pages as part of Figure 5.5.

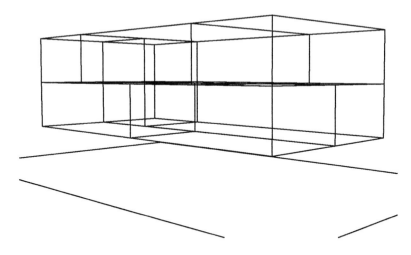

(a)   *Volume layout from building system*

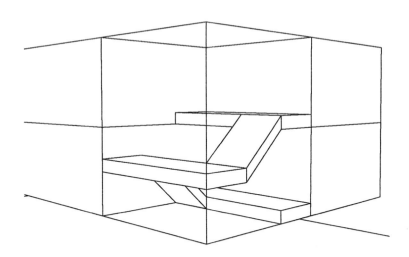

(b)   *Exterior view of staircase well*

Figure 5.5 *Sample output from LOKI system*

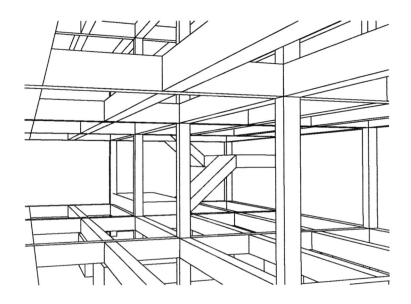

(c) *Interior view of structural frame*

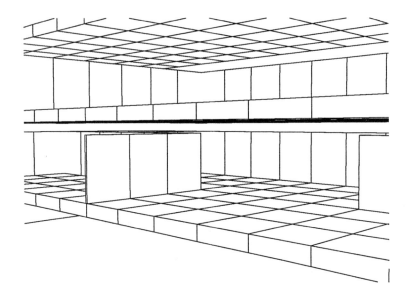

(d) *Interior view of internal walls and floors*

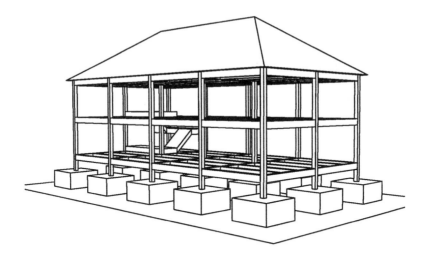

(e) *Structural frame prior to analysis*

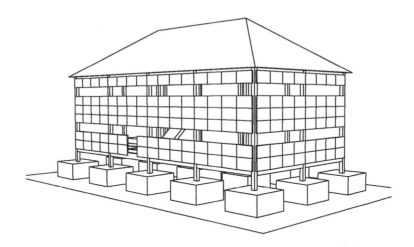

(f) *Exterior view of cladding option to building*

5.3 Applications in the construction industry

There are many areas where VR could immediately make an impact on the construction sector. Some of these relate to site operations and others aim to improve productivity in design. The areas mentioned in this section are summarised in Table 5.1. It is likely that the areas which will take up the technology most readily are the special application areas because there is a pressing need to develop safer methods of working in hazardous or hostile environments. Any technology which promises to remove humans from such places is always vigorously pursued. Once the applications are common in the specialist fields, it is likely that there will be a migration of the technology to wider construction use.

Area	Potential Applications
Site Operations	Rehearsing erection sequences Planning lifting operations Progress and monitoring Communications Inspection and maintenance Safety training and skills
Office Automation	Tele-conferences Project review and evaluation Project documentation Marketing
Design Phases	Preliminary and detailed design Lighting and ventilation simulations Data exchange Fire/safety/access assements Scheduling and progress reviews
Special Areas	Nuclear industry Subsea inspections and work Near space operations Micro inspection and testing

Table 5.1   *Potential applications of VR in construction*

5.3.1   Site operations

There are many areas on site which could benefit from the application of the VR technology outlined in the previous sections. Systems already exist for rehearsing erection sequences of complex facilities, but the interfaces to such systems are often clumsy and haphazard. Similarly, lifting operations from lorries and tower cranes could be rehearsed using a VR system well in advance of the actual event. Other applications include training and skills assessment. Also, if problems arose on site, a tele-presence system could give a site manager a better feel for the nature of the problem compared to a hastily scrawled note or garbled telephone conversation. Such tele-conferencing is already happening in some of the more progressive computer companies, but will also find a market on remote construction sites.

Lastly, work progress and schedules could be visualised by site staff if presented in a 3D format. A computer-generated model of the current state of the building could be used to compare where the site staff were working compared to where they should be according to the construction schedule [RETI90, SULL93].

5.3.2 Office automation

As mentioned above, tele-conferencing would find a ready market in construction not only on sites, but also for communication between far-flung design offices. Rather than exchanging paper drawings of the building, a situation is conceivable in which the building model could be passed between different members of a project design team. This would form the basis for a computer-generated walk-through of the site which the various designers could experience *en masse*. The scope for interacting with the model while trying to explain the effects of design changes would be invaluable as the effects would be immediately obvious to everyone using the model.

Similar immersions in the building model could be used as a marketing ploy to sell the buildings to potential clients. Likewise, they could be shown the construction sequence at different times and see how the constructors intend to erect 'their' building. There are tremendous implications for safety evaluations and cost efficiency in such a system. Lastly, a database of project documentation is feasible where documents are exchanged between people who meet as users of a common building model. Rather than exchanging a piece of paper on the real site, the electronic equivalent is passed between the users of the VR system and transformed into the right document by the database.

5.3.3 Conceptual and detailed design

As the examples in the figures show, the scope for VR to improve the visualisation of the building model is obvious. Using the data exchange medium of the MPCP, design changes can be made apparent to users in a way that is applicable to their needs and requirements. Services engineers could run their heating and lighting simulations and then display the results to the other members of the design team through a common VR model of the building. If any changes were to be made or cost restrictions imposed, the effects of these would become readily apparent to the observers. Much of this work could be done off-line but presented using the VR system.

Likewise, different building layouts could be evaluated by the designers or fire and safety issues could be examined. A VR model of a disabled person or wheelchair user could be constructed which simulated the effects of the disability by only allowing the user to move over gently inclined planes. This would emphasise to the designers the need for provision of improved access to most buildings. For example, the staircase of Figure 5.6 would be impractical for the user of a wheelchair.

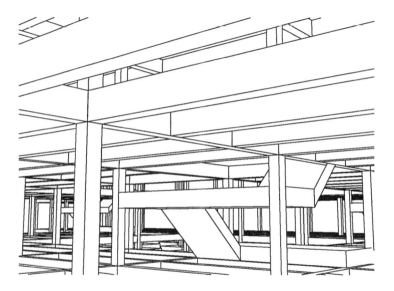

Figure 5.6 *Identification of access problems using VR*

Environmental impact assessments could be carried out using a VR system by interfacing the computer model to a discrete-event simulation system. Different alternatives for roads or railways could then be examined by non-expert users with more confidence than is currently the case. An application of this sort developed by the ABACUS unit at Strathclyde University could be used for environmental impact assessments. The researchers at ABACUS have constructed 3D surface models of areas of Edinburgh and Glasgow and can generate high-quality images from them. Their aim is to be able to import computer models of any recently proposed building developments and to assess the impact that the new structures will have on the immediate surroundings if they are allowed to proceed unmodified [COOM93].

5.3.4 *Special applications*

The last set of potential application areas have been grouped together because they share a common theme of hazard or danger to humans who would otherwise be called on to work in them. In the nuclear industry, there is a major problem with cleaning up after accidents or with decommissioning old reactors. In both cases, remote work vehicles are needed to prevent the human workers receiving fatal or damaging doses of radiation. In the past, remote operations have been carried out using single camera systems. It is a natural extension to adopt a tele-presence approach to vehicle control and so avoid the strain inherent in having to control a vehicle with little feedback from the environment. Likewise in the tunnelling industry, tunnel boring machines have become progressively more automated over the last ten years. It would be simple to implement a VR interface to the mechanisms which place tunnel segments or replace teeth on the shield face.

As with the nuclear industry, current control systems on submersible work vehicles could be usefully enhanced by the adoption of VR technology. This could be done by using force-reflecting manipulators which inform the operator of the forces that the robot is exerting. Much work that is done by divers could be carried out by remotely operated submersibles if the necessary investment in technology was made. Such investment has been made in the remote handling facilities developed by NASA for the Shuttle programme. Their new types of manipulator mimic the motions of the human operator and return information about the forces being exerted in the zero gravity conditions that facilitate satellite deliveries from the cargo bay of the shuttle orbiter. Other systems are being conceived for use on Mars when the telemetry delay can be of the order of several minutes.

5.4 Concluding remarks

This chapter has tried to demonstrate that there is potential for the application of VR technology in several areas in the construction industry, especially the design and erection of buildings. While the initial push for the technology will come from the more esoteric areas outlined in section 5.3.4, there is no reason why VR should not have a much wider impact. It is conceivable that data interchange and site meetings will be conducted through the medium of a 3D model of a building held within the VR system. The marketing and conceptual design areas of interest will be exploited as the technology offered by the vendors of computer graphics systems becomes cheaper and hence more accessible.

Initial research conducted has shown that it is possible to interface a VR workstation to a building design system and thence display the results of construction-oriented activity. The demonstration has also shown that the technology can be extended to many areas of interest such as vehicle control and simulation of real-world physics. In the future, it is hoped to build simulators of construction plant for training purposes which exploit the technology even further.

Remotely operated vehicles being driven from site offices many miles away from the workplace area are now technically possible, but it is unlikely that a safety-conscious industry would relinquish critical control of plant or machinery. However, a more immediate interface can be foreseen which improves worker productivity by putting them in the place of the machine or shows them exactly where to find their next working position. Shifting demographic trends are forcing up the average age of the workers and causing competition for the shrinking pool of younger workers. These two factors alone will ensure that the industry examines VR seriously in the coming decade.

5.5   Acknowledgements

The assistance of Dr Mike Griffin, Mr Dave Roberts and Mr Paul Sandoz of the Cybernetics Virtual Reality Research Group is gratefully acknowledged by the author. Figures 1 and 2 are copyright of the Cybernetics Virtual Reality Research Group.

References

ADEL88   Adeli H., An Overview of Expert Systems in Civil Engineering, in: Adeli H. (ed), Expert Systems in Construction and Structural Engineering, Chapman and Hall Ltd, London, 1988, pp 45-84.

ALCI89   Alciatore D.G., Hughes P.J., Traver A.E. and O'Connor J.T., Development and Simulation of an Ergonomic Control System for a Large Construction Manipulator. in: Proc 6th Int Symp on Automation and Robotics in Construction, San Francisco, Construction Industry Institute, 1989, pp 183-188.

ARC73   Applied Research of Cambridge Ltd, Computer-Aided Building: A Survey of Current Trends, ARC Ltd, Cambridge, 1973.

ATKI89   Atkin B.L., Atkinson P., Bridgewater C. and Ibanez-Guzman J., A New Direction in Automating Construction, in: Proc 6th Int Symp on Automation and Robotics in Construction, San Francisco, Construction Industry Institute, 1989, pp 119-216.

BERN89   Bernold L.E. and Abraham D.M., Control Systems for Computer Integrated Construction. in: Proc 6th Int Symp on Automation and Robotics in Construction, San Francisco, Construction Industry Institute, 1989, pp 228-236.

BIJL72   Bijl A., Application of CAAD Research in Practice: a System for House Design. in: Proc Int Conf on Comp in Arch, York, 1972, British Computer Society, London, 1972, pp 286-293.

BIJL79   Bijl A., Stone D. and Rosenstein D., Integrated CAAD Systems, Edinburgh Computer-Aided Architectural Design Studies, Final Report of DoE funded project DGR 470/12, March 1979, Edinburgh University, 1979.

BRAD91   Bradley D, Seward D and Garas F, Towards Site 2000, Developments in Automation and Robotics in Construction, Internal paper, University of Lancaster, 1991.

BRID90a   Bridgewater C. Atkin B., Atkinson P. and Ibanez-Guzman J., Parts-Set: Components for Modular Building Systems, in: Proc 7th Int Symp on Automation and Robotics in Construction, Bristol, June 1990, Bristol Polytechnic, 1990, pp 97-103.

BRID90b   Bridgewater C. Atkin B., Atkinson P. and Ibanez-Guzman J., MPCP: Computer Infrastructure for a Component-Based Building System, in: Proc 7th Int Symp on Automation and

Robotics in Construction, Bristol, June 1990, Bristol Polytechnic, 1990, pp 104-111.

BRID92   Bridgewater C., A new Approach to the Design of Buildings for Automated Construction, PhD Thesis, Departments of Engineering and Department of Construction Management & Engineering, University of Reading, UK, 1992.

BRID93   Bridgewater C. and Atkin B.L., Component Based Modular Building Design using Artificial Intelligence Techniques, in: Proc 4th EuropIA Conf, Design Research Centre, TU Delft, Delft, June, 1993.

BROW89   Brown M.A., Barriers to the Application of Robotics and High-Level Automation Within the UK Construction Industry, in: Proc 6th Int Symp on Automation and Robotics in Construction, San Francisco, Construction Industry Institute, 1989, pp 103-110.

BROW88   Browne J, Harhen J and Shivnan J, Production Management Systems: A CIM Perspective, Addison Wesley, London, 1988.

CSSC88   Centre for Strategic Studies in Construction, Building Britain: 2001, CSSC, Reading University, UK, 1988.

CSSC90   Centre for Strategic Studies in Construction, Building Towards 2001, CSSC, Reading University, UK, 1990.

COOM89a   Coomber M.J., Space Program, Building Magazine, 9 June 1989, Building (Pubs) Ltd, London, 1989, pp 72-73.

COOM89b   Coomber M.J., Through the Looking Glass, Building Magazine, 21 July 1989, Building (Pubs) Ltd, London, 1989, pp 50-51.

COOM89c   Coomber M.J., Rhapsody in Blue, Building Magazine, 21 July 1989, Building (Pubs) Ltd, London, 1989, p65.

COOM93   Coomber M.J., The Royal Mile Building Magazine, 04 July 1993, Building (Pubs) Ltd, London, 1993, pp 45-46.

DIST72   Distefano N. and Nagy D., Procedure in Building Methodology. in: Mitchell W.J. (ed), Proc EDRA3/AR8 Conf, Vol 2, UCLA, January 1972, University of California at Los Angeles, 1972.

DITL89   Ditlinger S. and Gates K., Animation/Simulation for Construction Planning and Scheduling, in: Proc 6th Int Symp on

Automation and Robotics in Construction, San Francisco, Construction Industry Institute, 1989, pp 491-498.

EAST72   Eastman C.M., General Space Planner: a System of Computer-Aided Architectural Design - User DocumentatioN, in: Mitchell W.J. (ed), Proc EDRA3/AR8 Conf, Vol 2, UCLA, January 1972, University of California at Los Angeles, 1972.

ELMS72   Elms D.G., A Comprehensive Computer-Aided Building Design System, Structures Publication No. 343, June 1972, MIT Report PB-212-615, R72-32, Massachusetts Institute of Technology for National Science Foundation, MIT, 1972.

FAZI89a   Fazio P., Zmeureanu R. and Kowalski A., Select-HVAC: KBS as an Advisor to Configure HVAC Systems, in: Computer-Aided Design, Vol 21, No. 2, March 1989, Butterworth and Co. (Pubs) Ltd, London, 1989.

FAZI89b   Fazio P., Bedard C. and Gowri K., Knowledge-Based System Approach to Building Envelope Design, in: Computer-Aided Design, Vol 21, No. 8, October 1989, Butterworth and Co. (Pubs) Ltd, London, 1989.

FENV90   Fenves S.J., Flemming U., Hendrickson C., Maher M.L. and Schmitt G., Integrated Software Environment for Building Design and Construction, in: Computer-Aided Design, Vol 22, No. 1, January 1990, Butterworth and Co. (Pubs) Ltd, London, 1990.

FINN88   Finn G.A., Expert systems Applications in Construction Engineering, in: Adeli H. (ed), Expert Systems in Construction and Structural Engineering, Chapman and Hall Ltd, London, 1988, pp 123-136.

FLEM88   Flemming U., Rule-Based Systems in Computer-Aided Architectural Design, in: Rychener M.D. (ed), Expert Systems for Engineering Design, Academic Press, London, 1988, pp 93-112.

FUKU88   Fukuda S., Codes and Rules and Their Roles as Constraints in Expert Systems for Structural Design, in: Adeli H. (ed), Expert Systems in Construction and Structural Engineering, Chapman and Hall Ltd, London, 1988, pp 309-322.

GRIF92   Griffin, M.P., A Cybernetic Perspective on Virtual Reality, PhD thesis, Department of Cybernetics, University of Reading, UK, 1992.

HOSK72   Hoskins E.M., OXSYS: An Integrated Computer-Aided Build-
           ing System for the Oxford Method, in: Proc Int Conf on Comp
           in Arch, York, 1972, British Computer Society, London,
           1972, pp 275-285.

IBAN90   Ibanez-Guzman J., Atkin B.L., Atkinson P., Bridgewater C.
           and Bayes J., Automation Systems and Robotic Tools for
           Modular Building Systems, in: Proc 7th Int Symp on Auto-
           mation and Robotics in Construction, Bristol, June 1990,
           Bristol Polytechnic, 1990, pp 87-96.

MAYE88   Mayer M.L., HI-RISE: An Expert System for Preliminary
           Structural Design, in: Rychener M.D. (ed), Expert Systems
           for Engineering Design, Academic Press, London, 1988, pp
           37-52.

MITC77   Mitchell W.J., Computer-Aided Architectural Design, Van
           Nostrand Reinhold, New York, 1977.

MYER75   Myer T.H., An Information System for Component Building,
           in: Eastman C.H. (ed), Spatial Synthesis in Computer-Aided
           Building, Applied Science Publishers, London, 1975, pp 41-
           66.

OLIV90   Oliver J.H. and Goodman E.D., Direct Dimensional NC
           Verification, in: Computer-Aided Design, Vol 22, No. 1,
           January 1990, Butterworth and Co. (Pubs) Ltd, London,
           1989.

PAEK90   Paek J. and Lovata N.L., Construction Information Systems:
           Integrating Data/Information Systems and Expert Systems,
           in: Proc 7th Int Symp on Automation and Robotics in Con-
           struction, Bristol, June 1990, Bristol Polytechnic, 1990, pp
           327-333.

RETI89   Retik A., Computer-Aided Design of Precast Building Sys-
           tem, in Proc Intl Conf on CADCAM and AMT in Israel,
           Jerusalem, December 1989, pp F4-1

RETI90   Retik A., Warszawski A., and Banai A., The Use of Computer
           Graphics as a Scheduling Tool, Building and Environment,
           25, No. 2, Pergamon Press, February 1990, pp 133-142.

RICH76   Richens P., New Developments in the OXSYS System, in:
           CAD-76, Proc 2nd Int Conf on Comp in Eng and Bldg Design,
           IPC Scientific and Technical Press, London, 1976, pp 44-50.

SEWA88   Seward D., Bradley D. and Bracewell R., The Development
           of Research Models for Automatic Excavation, in: 5th Int

Symp on Robotics in Construction, Tokyo, Japan Industrial Robot Association, 1988, pp 703-708.

SKIB88   Skibniewski, M.J., Robotics in Civil Engineering, Van Nostrand Reinhold, Wokingham, 1988.

SMIT89   Smithers T., AI-Based Design vs Geometry-Based Design, in: Computer-Aided Design, Vol 21, No. 3, April 1989, Butterworth and Co. (Pubs) Ltd, London, 1989.

STON86   Stone D., Building Regulations and Knowledge Based Systems, in: Hamilton G. and Wager D. (eds), Expert Systems for Construction and Services Engineering, Construction Industry Computing Association (CICA) & Building Services Research and Information Association (BSRIA), Cambridge, 1986.

SULL93   Sullivan R., Integration in Design and Simulation, in: Proc 10th Int Symp on Automation and Robotics in Construction, Construction Industry Institute, Texas, June, 1993, pp423-430.

SUTH68   Sutherland I.E., A Head-Mounted Three-Dimensional Display, in: Proc Fall Joint Conf on Computers, 33, pp 757-764, 1968.

WOHL89   Wohlford W.P., Griswold F.D. and Bode B.D., New Capability for Remote-Controlled Excavation, in: Proc 6th Int Symp on Automation and Robotics in Construction, San Francisco, Construction Industry Institute, 1989, pp 33-40.

YAMA90   Yamashita T. and Tsuchiya Y., Prefabrication of Reinforcing Bars Using CADCAM, in: Proc 7th Int Symp on Automation and Robotics in Construction, Bristol, June 1990, Bristol Polytechnic, 1990.

ZOZA89   Zozaya-Gorostiza C. Hendrickson C. and Reyhak D.R., Knowledge-Based Planning for Construction and Manufacturing, Academic Press Inc., London, 1989.

Chapter 6

Design by manufacture simulation using a glove input

D. Harrison, M. Jaques and P. Strickland

The link between designs, represented as geometric information, and a list of manufacturing instructions, has been a major obstacle to CAD/CAM integration. A number of techniques have developed to bridge this gap, including feature extraction and feature-based design methods. This chapter develops an alternative approach, first proposed by Gossard at M.I.T, in which, through designing parts by simulating manufacturing operations on the screen, the designer generates the manufacturing specification as he designs. A fast prototyping system has been developed using this approach, in collaboration with an automotive components supplier. This virtual manufacturing environment requires the designer to specify solutions in terms of manufacturing data, which are captured through glove input, by means of an interactive simulation of machining processes.

6.1   Introduction

Considerable research effort has been expended in an attempt to integrate design and manufacturing [CHOI85, SHAH88, PAND85]. Techniques based on feature extraction and feature-based modelling approaches have been extensively described in the literature [ALTI89]. However, these approaches have had limited success, either requiring input from a process planner after the design solution has been provided, or being applicable to only a restricted family of processes or components.

The alternative approach of 'Design by manufacturing simulation', as described by Jaques and Billingsley [JAQU91], overcomes many of these problems by requiring the designer to develop and specify solutions in terms of manufacturing data. These data are captured by means of an interactive simulation of manufacturing processes, in which the constraints of equipment, materials and tools are displayed to the designer. Figure 6.1 shows a comparison of the feature-based, feature extraction and design by manufacturing simulation approaches.

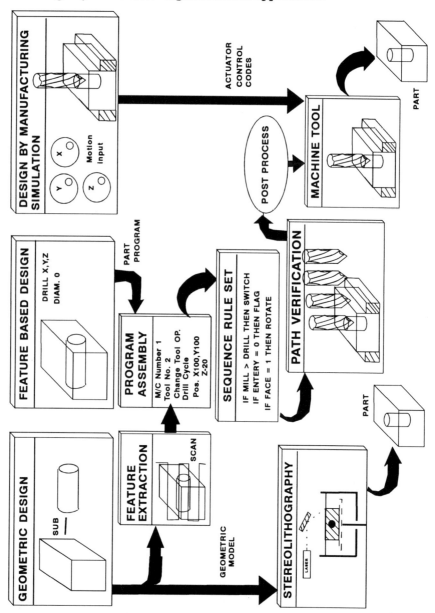

Figure 6.1   *Comparison of design approaches*

This chapter describes the application of the design by simulation approach to a fast prototyping system developed for the automotive component industry. Novel features of the system include the use of a glove to produce a more intuitive relationship between the designer and machine, and the simultaneous generation at design time of materials, costing and scheduling data, to support the implementation of concurrent engineering.

6.2   Design by manufacturing simulation (DMS)

Design by manufacturing simulation has its roots in the work of Gossard [GOSS75]. Gossard developed an analogic approach to numerical control (NC) part programming. He used hand cranks, similar to those used to control the slides of manual lathes, to control the position of a tool displayed via interactive graphics on a computer screen. The work centred around two-dimensional turning operations. As the tool was moved by the programmer, so the corresponding part shape change was displayed. The tool co-ordinates were displayed along with cut conditions, and this information was used to generate NC tape. This approach was referred to as 'part programming by doing'. Gossard suggested that this analogic approach could also be used as a means of design.

The ideas behind Gossard's work have been taken up by a number of authors, including Cutkosky and Tenebaum [CUTK90] and the work of Bowyer and Willis at Bath University [BOWY93] on 'virtual manufacturing' in a project to create a virtual mechanical engineering workshop.

Although these authors use a design by simulation approach, little information regarding materials handling, part manipulation, tooling or scheduling is generated by these simulations. We see one of the major benefits of our system as the generation of costing and scheduling data at design time.

6.3   Advantages of the DMS approach

The DMS approach is an ideal tool for the multidisciplinary teams necessary to implement concurrent engineering. Being a manufacturing-based rather than design-based tool, all areas are able to see the implications of their specification on the cost, lead time and quality of the product. The limitations and constraints of the equipment and materials can be considered simultaneously by the team. Thus the old-fashioned approach of design it first, ignoring the constraints, leaving the other departments to sort out the problems, can be replaced by a simultaneous, multidisciplinary approach. This approach should reduce product lead times and product costs.

6.4   The application of DMS to blanking and forming of metal strip

The industrial aim of the project is to reduce lead times on the design and manufacture of metal clips, produced by our collaborator, an automotive fastenings manufacturer. They have a product range of over 1000 variants, with present lead times, on average, of 6 weeks. The operations of one of their bending and forming machines has been simulated. Figure 6.2 shows a pneumatically driven tool and two sets of clamps for indexing the metal strip being controlled by the glove. This machine is being modified to numerical control and will act as a fast prototyping machine, using the output from our simulation.

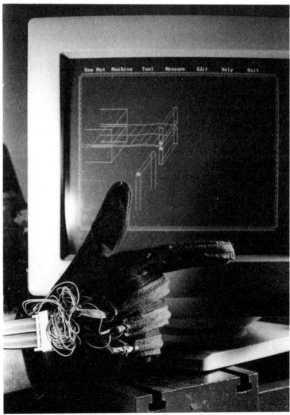

Figure 6.2   *Manufacturing simulation controlled by glove input*

6.5 The modelling method

After investigating the possibility of adapting existing commercial modelling packages, it was decided to develop an independent one dedicated to the machine simulation task. A geometric model is used to model the machines, tooling and raw material. The physical response of the raw material is modelled using finite element techniques.

Screen interaction between tools and material generates, through an interaction rule base, the mesh constraints which are sent to the finite element engine. This FE package then generates the nodal deflections of the material which are returned to the geometric modeller to modify the representation of the material. A schematic diagram of the system is shown in Figure 6.3.

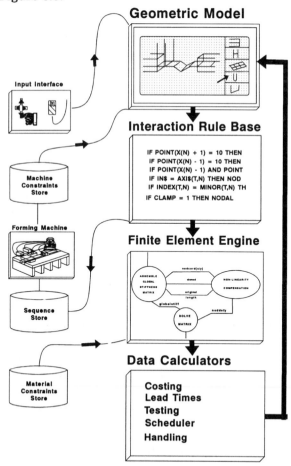

Figure 6.3 *DMS system architecture*

6.6   System overview

The implementation of manufacturing simulation in real time at a cost appropriate for the collaborating company presented a major challenge. The approach chosen for development was to use a 486 PC to run the geometric model, updated by a finite element engine running on a Meiko transputer computing surface. The use of multiple transputers on the Meiko computing surface allowed us to exploit the inherent parallelism of the task to increase the speed of the finite element calculations. For the target system a 486 PC with a Fast Nine transputer card installed will be used.

6.7   Gloves as intuitive input devices

'Design by manufacturing simulation' infers that 'design' is being carried out on the screen. However, most CAD systems are not equipped with the intuitive human computer interfaces necessary to conceptualise a design. The awkward nature of many human interfaces prevents the designer from easily creating and modifying designs.

Filerman and Ulrich [FILE89] suggest that design quality and individual designer productivity could be substantially increased if CAD systems were equipped with more intuitive input devices. They proposed that an input device that exploits human tactile and spatial reasoning abilities would be more intuitive than current interfaces. They suggested that if a mechanical designer could physically manipulate an intuitive input device in the same way as an artist or designer would work with clay, then they could rapidly conceptualise a design and easily iterate through many design options. They proposed a form of 'electronic clay' which would permit this interaction. The idea of 'electronic clay' has potential for geometric design systems. However, perhaps the most appropriate input for manufacturing simulations would be mock ups of the normal machine controls themselves. This was the approach taken by Gossard in his original work in analogic programming.

Through using a glove as input to our system we hoped to improve the correspondence between the designers hand operations and the modelling operations of the system. Initial control of the clamps and the forming tool was by manipulating cursor keys. A glove input device and an ultrasonic hand tracker, originally constructed for a sign language recognition project, were interfaced to the DMS system to investigate more intuitive control.

The system was configured so that intuitive gestures for move left, move right, move up, move down (such as might be adopted instinctively for controlling a backing car or a swinging crane) could be used to guide

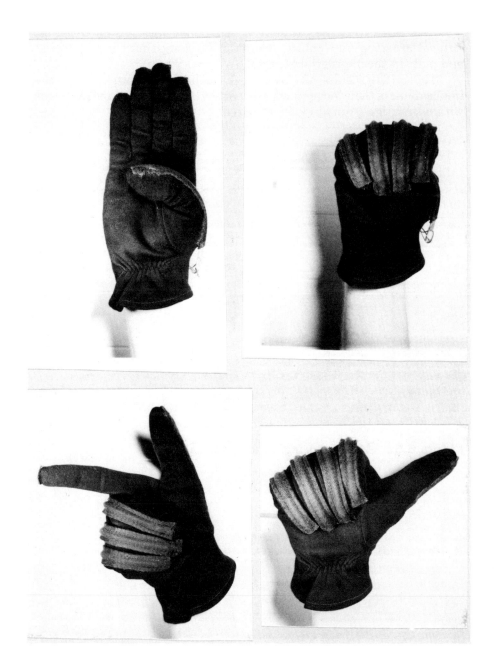

Figure 6.4   *Up, down, left and right gestures*

the machine tool. Figure 6.4 shows the gestures used to control the axes of the machine. Work is continuing on using the tracker system to permit natural 'grasping' and 'pulling' operations to clamp the strip of material and pull out the appropriate length.

The initial results of glove use have been encouraging, but the implications of their longer term use, particularly in the light of problems with user fatigue, remain to be explored.

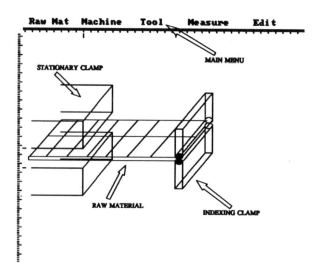

Figure 6.5a   *Material being drawn from coil*

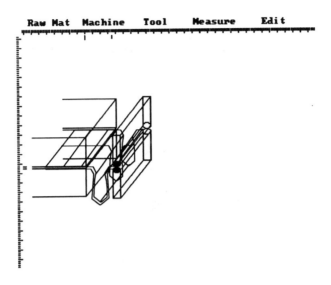

Figure 6.5b *Buckling due to axail load*

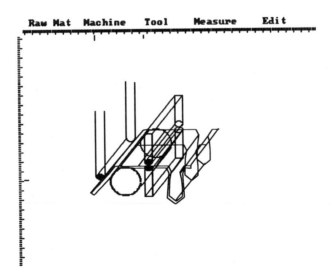

Figure 6.5c *Forming of tab by perpendicular load*

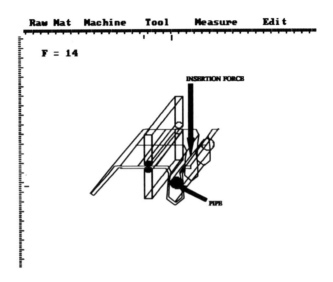

Figure 6.5d   *Testing insertion force*

6.8   Results

The system has been used to sucessfully design several clip variants. The process is outlined below:

Figure 6.5a shows the raw material strip being pulled from the stationary clamp by the indexing clamp. The user selects the indexing clamp, which appears at its home position, they then open the jaws, by making the 'up' gesture, Figure 6.4. The user then indexes the clamp to the left and closes it to grip the material, by using the 'right' gesture the material is pulled through the stationary jaws. Figure 6.5b shows the material buckling due to an axial compressive load applied by the indexing clamps, the stationary clamp having been closed. In Figure 6.5c a former is introduced and the operator is now controlling the tool which is indexed to the right, from its home position. Once in position the tool is lowered, as it contacts the material so a perpendicular load is applied and the material bends. Figure 6.5d shows the user testing the insertion force of the clip by moving a model of the part (in this case a brake pipe) and loading it till the clip deflects sufficiently to allow the pipe to enter.

6.9   Discussion

The DMS approach is undoubtedly open to criticism. Comments have included that it is not how designers design, that construction is a separate process to design, that some practical aspects are not relevant during the creative part of design and that design should be imagination limited, not machining limited. These and similar questions are considered at length in Cutkosky and Tenebaum [CUTK90].

On the question of whether attention to manufacturing processes during design reduces creativity, Cutkosky and Tenebaum quote an experienced model maker, who said "I often design while I am fabricating. For me, holding a piece of metal or plastic suggests solutions. I don't know where that sensitivity, that empathy for the material comes from, but I think that if one is just trained in the equations of the material properties without having physically manipulated them, one misses a lot of intuitive design opportunities".

They also argue that rapid prototyping fosters creativity, and that adding extra (relaxable) constraints is a good way to stimulate thought.

Our view at this stage is DMS provides a useful tool for the fast prototyping of simple designs. A design space restricted by manufacturing constraints is faster to explore and, if a solution can be found, the result is often cheaper and simpler than was originally contemplated. The extension of this technique to broader design problems awaits further improvements in both human computer interfaces and speed/cost trade offs in modelling and simulation.

In DMS it is essential that the characteristics of materials and processes should be incorporated into the user interface to capture the feel of the operation. The challenge is that the representation of these characteristics must be fast and flexible if it is not to hinder the designer. To increase the speed of the process it is vital to find the right level of abstraction for representing the process. It must capture the essential characteristics and constraints without too much detail. The level of abstraction used in our case has to a large extent been dictated by the requirement of the collaborators that the system be portable and the consequent restriction to PC based technology.

6.10   Conclusions

Although 'design' in our system has many limitations, the system does provide a useful tool for the detailed design of components formed from metal strip. Potentially the system could reduce the design lead times from 6 weeks to as little as 6 hours. The system works for detailed design, with a designer already committed to a manufacturing process and a particular manufacturing facility. However, without extensive trials, it is difficult to judge whether in general designers will find DMS a good way to design, or whether it will enhance or reduce creativity. At present the system is best regarded as a high level process planning tool, which, through generation of costing and manufacturing data at design time, is able to reduce product lead times. It is hoped that further improvements in interfacing and in speed of operation will lead to it eventually supporting true conceptual design.

The advantage of working in metal forming has been that the range of operations to consider has been relatively small. However, sheet metal processing , along with injection moulding and machining, accounts for a large fraction of the fabrication processes for engineered artifacts, and thus the implementation of DMS for metal forming is an important contribution to the development of a virtual mechanical engineering workshop, such as that proposed by Bowyer [BOWY93].

References

CHOI85   CHOI, B. and BARASH, M., "STOPP: an approach to CADCAM integration", Computer Aided Design, 1985, 17, (4), pp.162-168.

SHAH88   SHAH, J. and ROGERS, M., "Functional requirements and conceptual design of the feature-based modelling systems", Computer-Aided Engineering Journal, 1988, 5, (1), pp.9-15.

PAND85   PANDE, S. and PALSULE, N., "GCAPPS-a computer-assisted generative process planning system for turned components", Computer-Aided Engineering Journal., 1988, 5, (4), pp.163-168.

ALTI89   ALTING, L. and ZHANG, H. "Computer Aided Process Planning:the state-of-the-art survey", International Journal of Production Research, 1989, 27, (4), pp.553-585.

JAQU91   JAQUES, M. and BILLINGSLEY, J. and HARRISON, D. "Generative feature-based design-by-constraints as a means of integration within the manufacturing industry", Computer-Aided Engineering Journal, Dec., 1991,18,(6),pp.261-267.

GOSS75   GOSSARD, D., "Analogic part programming with interactive graphics", PhD Dissertation, 1975, Massachusetts Institute of Technology, USA.

CUTK90   CUTKOSKY, M. and TENEBAUM, J., "A methodology and computational framework for concurrent product and process design", Mechanism and machine theory, 1990, 25, (3), pp.365-38.

BOWY93   BOWYER, A. and WILLIS, P., "Design by Virtual Manufacturing", SERC, ACME Status Reports on Research Funded By The Directorate, 1993, U.K.

FILE89   FILERMAN, M. and Ulrich, K., "Issues in the design of tactile input devices for mechanical CAD systems", Proceedings of the IEEE International Conference on Systems, Man and Cybernetics, 1989, Vol 3, pp 1087-1088.

Chapter 7

Real applications – virtual markets (selling the vision of virtual reality)

R. Stone and A. Connell

7.1   Introduction

As any European virtual reality researcher or developer will know, selling the vision and technical potential of virtual reality to a sceptical and money-conscious market can prove to be a highly challenging and sometimes frustrating exercise. The misleading promises surrounding VR, fuelled by the media and the entertainments industry, have been, without doubt, the cause of most of the frustration, leading to a widespread perception that the state of the art in VR is very poor indeed. The effect of the VR "hype" was that, until recently, many potential industrial users openly declared that they would never contemplate procuring a "child's game" for serious commercial applications. Having raised the hopes of other, more enthusiastic sponsors, the misleading statements about what VR technology could already achieve produced serious disappointment once they had experienced the primitive graphics and display technology first hand.

National and European research bodies responsible for promoting new technologies in, for example, the fields of information technology, robotics and medicine have not been proactive in co-ordinating efforts in VR, due partly to a selfish refusal to employ qualified consultants (relying almost solely upon in-house and ill-informed personnel) and partly to the now-monotonously used excuse of "internal reorganisation". One well-known person within the CEC has said on many an occasion that specific technological developments are not what European research institutions should be concentrating on. Content (whatever this means) should be the focus of VR endeavours. Europe has, historically, been very successful at adapting new technologies – artificial intelligence, multimedia, neural networks – to serious applications. Yet, after witnessing the chaos caused by the collapse of one US company in 1992 (VPL Inc.), with distributors of other non-European equipment subsequently failing to cope with the resultant market demand, one must question the impact of such a volatile market on Europe's ability to deliver results of use by industry. The lack of technologies indigenous to the European VR market, together with the reproduction of effort throughout the continent, particularly in the academic arena, has not helped the maturation process of VR, as evidenced by a distinct absence of industrial uptake.

Fortunately, things are now changing, and the scene is perhaps set for a maturation of VR technology between now and 1995. However, to address the "state of the art" in VR in a paper to be presented 2–3 months hence, would be as foolhardy as stating in the spring of 1992 that real-time near-photorealism was more than 5 years into the future. The general state of the art in VR has, perhaps, been best catalogued in some of the more recent books on the subject, such as Kalawsky [KALA93], Earnshaw et al. [EARN93], Aukstakalnis [AUKS93], Thompson [THOM93] and Pimental & Teixiera [PIME92]. Also, there is a wealth of information on contemporary technologies in such journals and newsletters as *Presence, Virtual Reality Systems, Virtual Reality News* (UK and USA) and *CyberEdge*, to mention but a few. Nevertheless, in certain areas, most notably real-time graphics capability, the technologies underpinning VR have reached a level whereby credibility and respectability for the field is growing in industrial and commercial circles.

7.2   The problems

In the early days of the evolution of the European VR "community", one of the prime movers was, without doubt, W Industries, based in Leicester. The emergence of the Virtuality Games System was accompanied not only by Hollywood-style product launch events, but also by much speculation about the role VR would play in the future of computing technology.

Researchers already involved in the field of VR in the UK and elsewhere were, naturally, quite keen to use the Virtuality System as the test bed for their own endeavours. Many simply wanted to obtain the Visette head-mounted display, rather than having to rely on home-built LCD (liquid crystal display) headsets, or on the VPL EyePhone models 1 or 2. The Visette appeared, at the time, to offer an attractive alternative to the American products, especially given that the early papers presented by W Industries' personnel made much of the use of "independent experts" who had been contracted by W Industries to provide advice on human factors, health and safety issues, particularly in the development of the Visette. Despite an interest in procuring individual parts of the Virtuality System, W Industries was only concerned with whole-system sales, and was not prepared to release the Visette for research and development purposes. Even for those who were interested in complete VR systems, it was soon discovered that W Industries had adopted all manner of techniques to ensure that the Virtuality architecture was closed and therefore neither adaptable nor programmable by purchasers. This meant that the system was unusable as a means of demonstrating a variety of potential applications, unless, of course, W Industries was contracted to program the application itself.

This "closed shop" syndrome not only applied to specific commercial sensitivities, but also to the myriad of hardware platforms, data input and display peripherals and software toolkits currently available and planned for the future. Virtual reality is concerned first and foremost with intuitive, real-time interaction with three-dimensional computer-generated graphics. Consequently, developments in the field are not only restricted to the use of systems hosting immersion peripherals, such as stereoscopic headsets and gloves.

7.3   Displays

Display products becoming available both to industry and the general public take the form of "desktop" and workstation configurations, using monitors which vary in quality from VGA standard with PC systems to high-resolution screens such as those used with Silicon Graphics and Evans & Sutherland platforms. Other more specialised display systems include multiple TV monitors (as used in some "location-based entertainment" VR centres and on the British Broadcasting Corporation TV programme Cyberzone), counterbalanced monoscopic and stereoscopic viewers (e.g. LEEP Systems' Cyberface 3, or Fake Space Labs/Division Inc's Binocular Omni-Orientable Monitor, BOOM), liquid crystal field sequential spectacles, Barco/Sony video projectors and passive stereoscopic techniques (i.e. using polarised filter pairs on proprietary video projectors and viewing glasses). The stereoscopic headset situation is due to improve dramatically between the date of publication of this book and the opening months of 1994. Efforts in the USA and Europe are now concentrating on the use of miniature cathode ray tubes. For example, undaunted by the problems of trading and supply in a very volatile VR market during late 1992 and the first 5 months of 1993, the small American Company of Virtual Research ceased supply of its popular Flight Helmet system and concentrated efforts on a new head-mounted display for launch this summer. Codenamed the Eyegen 3, the headset is a lightweight mount, housing 2 monochrome CRTs (cathode ray tubes) with colour wheels. Initial specifications are:

- Resolution of 369,750 colour elements (123,250 triads) – 250 resolvable lines x 493 NTSC lines x 3 colours

- Field of view of 40° diagonal @ 100% overlap; 48° @ 50% overlap

- Interpupillary adjustment, plus individual CRT focus wheels and display housing spring release

- Ratchet headband with 2 adjusters

- 0.69 kg headset; 0.35 kg cable drag

- Sennheiser high-fidelity stereo headphones

- Mounting for all commercial spatial tracking systems.

Another system, to be featured at the 1993 Siggraph convention in Anaheim is n-Vision's new Datavisor 9c. This headset, based on Tektronix NuColor LCD shutter devices, boasts resolutions up to 1280 x 960 at 30Hz, with a monocular field of view of 50°. The 13" x 12" x 5.25" headset features inter-pupillary adjustment of between 58mm and 78mm, with a weight of 3.2lbs. Optional equipment includes headphones, a microphone and a novel bladder fitting system for environments where rapid movements or shocks are likely.

In Europe, a small Dutch company called Virtual Interfaces has been committed to producing a VR headset indigenous to the continent. There is no trade name for the company's headset at the time of writing, but the initial specifications claim "far above VGA" resolution. Other independent comments suggest that the head-mount structure is quite impressive, and that illumination, contrast, brightness and colour saturation features are good. The headset design is based on a pair of 1.5" CRTs with Tektronix colour shutters, with the optical assembly due for testing at the beginning of June, 1993. Other initial specifications are:

- Field of view of 57°, fully overlapped

- Raster area: 28 x 22 mm, resolution: 880 lines

- Line width (at 50% intensity): 880 lines

- Exit pupil: 18 mm, with an eye relief of 28 mm

- Linearity: <2%; Vignetting: 75%

- Adjustments for interocular distance and head height and width

These are but three of a probable catalogue of nearly 20 LCD/CRT headset systems which will come into existence over the next year or so, many of which will be featured in prototype form at Siggraph 1993. Whilst the search for new and better quality headset designs is to be applauded, the transition from LCD to the higher energy CRT devices, mounted around the head (i.e. close to the temporal lobes of the brain), together with their typical arrangement of narrow field-of-view optics, opens up a whole new set of health and safety problems which must be addressed.

7.4 Data input devices

Available data input devices for VR systems are also many and varied. The most common form of device used in immersive VR consists of a spatial tracker embedded within a low-cost hand grip or modified PC games joystick (e.g. the ARRL Teletact Commander, the KAT keyboard, the Cricket etc.). These hand grips have become popular over the last 12–18 months, due to the high cost and lack of reliability of glove-based products. As mentioned above, in November 1992, and for a variety of political and technology supply reasons, VPL Inc., until then the world's major supplier of VR hardware and software, collapsed. This event had a "knock-on" effect across the globe, with distributors of competing products experiencing considerable difficulties in responding to a rapidly expand-ing market, particularly in Europe. The only other supplier of a glove-based interaction system for VR was Virtex in the USA. Following the collapse of VPL, the price of their CyberGlove system increased from around $US 6000 to $US 14,000! Fortunately, new glove products are beginning to emerge. The GLAD-IN-ART glove is an excellent example of a complete input-feedback system. Other good examples include the Cardiff (UK)-based TCAS Ltd conductive elastomer glove and another British product, the "SmartGlove". Tactile and force feedback systems, together with replication of other skin-mediated senses, still present the VR community with a major challenge, although there are considerable efforts across the globe addressing proportional pneumatics, exoskeletons, vibratory trans-ducers, shape memory alloys and electromechanical back-driveable joysticks.

One potentially exciting area in the field of data input systems design for VR is that of "biocontrol". The term biocontrol refers to the recording of bioelectric or electrophysiological signals, originating naturally from processes within the human body (e.g. muscle and nerve activity), which, suitably filtered and amplified, can be used to control other processes, remote from the originating human body (internal bodily processes can also be controlled to some extent, as with biofeedback training). Until quite recently, biocontrol has been believed to be of interest to followers of science fiction. However, due to relatively new developments, originally designed for seriously handicapped individuals, biocontrol is now being investigated in laboratories researching virtual reality and telepresence.

Anecdotal reports from the USA suggest that already, electrophysiological signals are being used to control motion through generated worlds, to identify individual finger movements (in an attempt to replace gloves as input devices) and to control telerobots. It has not been possible to verify these claims before the publication of the final version of this chapter. Nevertheless, it was felt that, for completeness, mention of what might become a rapidly expanding area of scientific interest should be included. In the summer of 1992, Biocontrol Systems of Palo Alto, USA, released a number of alpha test units of their Biomuse system, a recording and control package, for around $US 10,000. Sense8's WorldToolKit for run-time VR world generation incorporates a device driver package for the Biomuse technology. Biomuse is a special purpose signal processing computer that detects low-level electrical signals from small disk sensors placed around the human body (e.g. around the eyes, over large muscles or on the scalp). The system is designed around a Texas Instruments processor which analyses the filtered and amplified signals. The hardware permits the recording of signals in up to 8 channels and is linked to a host computer by means of an RS232 serial port. Another product due for release in 1992 is known as Eyecon, described loosely as an eye-controlled joystick/mouse system (cf. eye tracking technologies). Many human factors projects associated with virtual environments (e.g. advanced fighter cockpit designs) are evaluating the use of eye movement and changes in eye characteristics as a means of control and mental workload estimation, respectively. In much the same way as speech recognition is occasionally considered as a "hands-free" form of control, so too is eye tracking.

There are a number of ways in which the eye may be tracked. The most popular involves the use of infra-red LEDs (light-emitting diodes) and the reflection of IR (infra-red) off the sclera (or "white") of the eye. A recent development in this sort of approach is a system known as Eyegaze. Eyegaze uses an infra-red diode, mounted coaxially with a video camera to illuminate the cornea of the eye, generating an effect similar to "red-eye" with amateur flash photography, when the flash bulb is too close to the camera lens. This brightening of the eye is exploited by an image processing system which calculates and tracks the centre of the pupil. One of the more accurate but highly intrusive methods involves the implanting of a metallic coil in the cornea of the eye for the purposes of electro-magnetic tracking. Commercially, eye tracking equipment is available. However, there is some evidence that current head-mounted eye tracking equipment is inherently unreliable and requires frequent recalibration due to the slippage of the headgear. For the foreseeable future, and until a reliable and low-cost method of integrating such devices within commercial VR headsets is achieved, eye tracking will remain as a means of display evaluation in research laboratories.

7.5 Computing platforms

Computing platforms have, since RB2 (Reality Built for 2) – VPL's mainstream virtual reality system – developed in many forms to support both immersive and non-immersive VR. As far as British developments in computing systems for VR are concerned, the two key players in this respect have been Dimension International and Division Limited.

Dimension International has been the driving force behind the Virtual Reality Toolkit (or "Superscape") product, currently a non-immersive VR platform hosted on an IBM 486PC clone running at 33 or 66MHz. The graphical output is handled by a SPEA Fire graphics card coupled to a high definition monitor. The main input devices to the system are a Spaceball 6-degrees-of-freedom controller, and a standard mouse (although some UK institutions have investigated the interfacing of other VR peripherals, such as gloves). The front end of the Dimension package consists of three main environments: a Shape editor, a World editor and a Visualiser. In the Shape editor, objects are created in 3D. In the World editor, pre-defined shapes are placed in their world coordinates. Dimension's Visualiser allows the user to move around and interact with the virtual world, taking commands from the spaceball or mouse. Version 3 of Superscape supports limited texturing and a form of 3D sound.

Division Limited, a company based in North Bristol (UK) with distributors throughout Europe, was recently floated on the UK stock exchange, and has been pioneering the use of transputer and i860 technologies in its development of the Vision range of products. These products are based on modular and high speed graphics engines which, it is claimed, together with the systems' client-server or actor-director architectures, avoid the processing bottlenecks associated with conventional approaches to generating and interacting with virtual worlds. Until recently, Division's most advanced in-house development was based on a next generation virtual reality system called SuperVision, based on a scalable communications architecture called a High Speed Link (HSL; 200 Mbytes per second). SuperVision has been designed, it is claimed, to support parallel vision applications of the sort required by many serious applications. ARRL procured Division's first ever Vision system and, in 1992, commissioned the company to provide an upgraded version of the more powerful SuperVision engine. Division's dVS operating system was recently ported onto Silicon Graphics architecture, in an attempt to exploit the more powerful graphics rendering capability of that company's machines.

Despite the reasonable achievements of these two British companies, many users of advanced graphics systems still prefer to pursue a course which, whilst more expensive, delivers a proven and industry-standard platform. In this respect, it has been known for some time that Silicon Graphics (SG) would eventually target the virtual reality "market" with a professional product that would compete seriously in terms of performance and price with existing platforms and produce virtual images of acceptable quality to industry, especially when combined with the model building and run-time virtual world generation power of software packages, such as ModelGen/MultiGen and Sense8's WorldToolKit. SG's Crimson RealityEngine did just this, with many of the functions provided in software form on other platforms, integrated on hardware on the SG system. This provided the capability to handle much larger and more visually complex worlds – with a stereoscopic display and potential multi-user capability. The RealityEngine has been described as the third generation of IRIS graphics supercomputer, giving real time graphics performance through the use of Mips RISC R3000 or R4000 processors. Some of the key features of the RealityEngine Architecture include:

- High performance anti-aliasing (up to 16 sub-samples per pixel)

- Standard 4MBytes of on-line texture memory (giving up to 380, 128x128 simultaneous mapped textures)

- Photographic texturing (1024x1024 textured elements maximum), projected and 3D texturing capability

- Multiple channel outputs (e.g. up to 12 low resolution channels, or up to four 1280x1024-resolution channels per system, allowing multi-participant interaction with virtual worlds)

- Up to 32bit Z buffer for all hidden line removal operations

- Animation sequences using texture and geometry

- Lightpoint support; steerable independent spotlights with user-definable lobe shape

- User-definable video formats (including RGB, VGA, PAL, NTSC, High-Definition TV)

Launched in the UK in the spring of 1993, Silicon Graphics' Onyx graphics "supercomputer" uses up to twenty-four 150MHz MIPS R4400 processors in a single enclosure. Onyx systems are available with RealityEngine2 graphics subsystems. RealityEngine2 is an enhanced version of the RealityEngine graphics subsystem (described above), featuring performance of up to 2 million t-mesh polygons and 320M textured, anti-aliased pixels a second. Real-time multi-sample anti-aliasing, advanced stereo capabilities, 96-bit colour, volume rendering and 32-bit Z-buffer are just a few of the many features shared by both the VTX and RealityEngine2 graphics subsystems.

Every Onyx graphics supercomputer offers a flexible frame-buffer architecture that allows for software-selection of display resolutions and even multiple outputs from a single RealityEngine2 or VTX graphics pipeline. When used with the multichannel option, RealityEngine2-equipped systems can support dual high-resolution screens, or up to six 640 x 480 outputs. Both graphics subsystems support resolutions from VGA up to 1280 x 1024, while RealityEngine2 subsystems (with the optional Raster Manager board) are capable of 1600 x 1200, 1920 x 1035, 1920 x 1152 and other high resolution formats. Onyx systems include composite video output and genlock, so an area of interest from the high resolution monitor can be output to a standard NTSC or PAL videocassette.

In what could become a long-standing price/performance battle between the world's graphics and simulation giants, on October 20th 1992, Evans & Sutherland Computer Corporation and Sun Microsystems Computer Corporation introduced a 3D graphics accelerator family for the SPARC/Solaris platform. Designed, no doubt, to compete ultimately with Silicon Graphics RealityEngine series, the "stereo ready" Freedom family of accelerators claims to deliver the industry's fastest graphics, offering over twice the 3D graphics speed of any other workstation. This partnership is definitely one to watch over the coming years, as is the price/performance competition. SG have stated that, within two years, the power of the Onyx will be available at a desk-top price and within a desk-top tower enclosure.

Other companies have attempted to produce VR computing systems or dedicated add-on boards, but have met with limited success, some even collapsing, thereby leaving many purchasers of graphics boards with non-standard, non-upgradeable hardware and software. Many companies seem to be obsessed with pushing their hardware and/or software product to become the "European Standard". If there is one thing the continent does not need yet, it is standards for operating systems, toolkits and hardware. Data interchange protocols, yes (e.g. the ISO/ESPRIT STEP Initiative); human factors standards, definitely; but not systems standards forced upon the European VR Community through commercial greed rather than technical rationale. Until the volatile VR market actually settles down (and many believe this will not happen in Europe until post-1995), there can be no guarantee that any one product line – hardware or software – will emerge as the *de facto* standard. For many, if not all, VR applications outside the leisure and entertainment industry, it is not satisfactory to consider just one company's system or one form of peripheral data input/data display equipment. If one does then one risks falling prey to the "closed shop" syndrome – irreplaceable or non-upgradeable hardware and non-portable software. The international VR product range – and therefore the "state of the art" – is changing and growing all the time.

7.6   Industrial applications: credibility at last?

State of the art is one thing. Actual commercial and industrial take-up is very much another. In the introduction to this chapter, it was pointed out how challenging yet frustrating selling virtual reality to industry and commerce can be. Yet, in the United Kingdom, endeavours for serious commercial VR applications have, over the past year, received a number of welcome boosts. Not only has Division Limited been floated on the stock exchange (with shares more than doubling in value on the launch date of 17 May), but also Europe's largest commercial project to date was initiated in May without national government or CEC support! The project, called VRS (virtual reality & simulation), is led by Advanced Robotics Research Limited. The aim of VRS, initially planned as a two-year programme of work, is not only to keep British industry abreast of significant international developments in the field, but also to demonstrate to participating companies the commercial value of virtual reality and simulation. At the end of the two-year programme, VRS will provide the participating companies with sufficient know-how to introduce the technologies into their own businesses with minimal technical and financial risk.

VRS is an initiative fully funded by British industry. Companies were invited to join the programme on one of four tiers, depending on their perceived role: Full, Technology Watch, Small/Medium Enterprise (SME) or Associate Membership. Full membership has been taken up by those companies which already have a well-defined application and wish to sponsor a demonstration of the application using ARRL's VR and simulation resources. Technology watch is a grade of membership designed to accommodate those companies who wish to keep a close watching brief on short-term developments within VRS, prior to choosing an application of their own. The SME grade of membership was offered to two local companies involved in civil engineering and architectural practice. At the date of publication of this book, the VRS membership list included the following:

Bell Northern Research (Northern Telecom)

British Nuclear Fuels plc

GEC Alsthom Engineering Systems Limited (Whetstone)

Hunting Engineering Limited (Ampthill)

ICI Chemicals & Polymers Limited (Runcorn)

M W Barber Group Limited (Romiley, Stockport)

Multi-Design Consultants Limited (Stockport)

North West Water Group (Warrington)

Rolls-Royce plc (Derby)

United Kingdom Nirex Limited (Harwell)

University of Salford (Department of Surveying)

Vickers Shipbuilding and Engineering Limited (Barrow-In-Furness)

Westlakes Research Institute (Cumbria)

Associate VRS members are companies and institutions which bring important hardware and software products and information services to the project. The current list includes:

- The British Library Document Supply Centre (The library has recently established an important VR database facility at Boston Spa, one which will not only bring information benefits to VRS collaborators, but will itself benefit from ARRL's national and international activities)

- CIMIO Limited (CIMIO is a particularly important associate member, as the company, based in Surrey, UK, is actively involved in the ISO/ESPRIT STEP (STandard for the Exchange of Product model data) initiative, concerning computer-aided design format translation and data exchange software/standards)

- Deneb Robotics Inc (A Michigan-based company, suppliers of IGRIP and QUEST VR and simulation software)

- Silicon Graphics Computers Limited (suppliers of high-performance graphics workstations, such as the RealityEngine2 or Onyx System currently in place at Salford)

- Transformation Software Limited (Thame-based European distributors of the American company Software Systems' MultiGen and ModelGen visual simulation and VR software)

- TCAS Limited (Cardiff-based developers of interactive gloves and controllers for robotics and VR applications)

- Virtual Presence Limited (London-based distributors of the American company Sense8's WorldToolKit and other hardware/software for VR applications)

Two studies already underway are being carried out for Rolls-Royce and UK Nirex. Whilst specific technical details about the work cannot be released, for reasons of confidentiality, the Nirex project relates to the development of a virtual model of the Deep Waste Repository currently being considered for the safe and cost effective disposal underground of solid low and intermediate level radioactive wastes at Sellafield. The requirements envisaged for such a model are twofold, namely:

(a)   to permit investigations of virtual reality (VR) technologies for such purposes as interactive design and visualisation and training procedures. These investigations would employ the basic UK NIREX Repository computer model constructed using a variety of standard computer-aided design and VR graphics rendering packages. An important aspect of this requirement is that changes to the graphical model and its components must be efficiently supported, to occur in line with the phased development of the Repository. Commencement of operations is scheduled for the next century, with a subsequent operational period of 50 years.

(b)   using the same model database, to provide the foundation for producing a commercial video, for initial screening at a planning application meeting involving UK NIREX personnel, relevant planning authorities and, possibly, members of the general public.

The collaborative link between the work of ARRL in virtual reality and Rolls-Royce plc in aircraft engine design and construction began in earnest following a meeting between the two companies on 8 April 1992. At that meeting, the future potential for using VR to compliment computer-aided design activities (based on the CADDS4X Package) within Rolls-Royce's digital pre-assembly – DPA – department was discussed, especially with regard to the problem of assessing maintenance issues. Physical mock-ups of aircraft engines – in this specific instance the Trent 800 system for the Boeing 777 – can cost millions of pounds to fabricate, yet it is during the fabrication process that some problems of maintainability become apparent. In particular there are those problems which may arise due to the limitations of conventional CAD workstations to provide their users with an "intuitive" or natural view of the engine and its components. VR was considered to offer a logical design step between the DPA CAD modelling activities and mock-up fabrication phases. "Immersees" could experience the service layout of an engine and could provide an early assessment of the planned distribution of services – pipework, gearboxes, brackets and so on – for their ease of maintainability.

The majority of the early work, then, centred on the conversion of data from Rolls-Royce's CADDS4X System into a form compatible with the Division SuperVision operating system. Due to the complex interpositions between elements of the converted Trent model, the pipework assembly was found to generate excellent stereoscopic images, even using commercial LCD headsets used in VR. However, the polygonal nature of the model lacked a degree of professionalism and interaction with the pipework – withdrawing individual elements using ARRL's Teletact Commander hand grip – was not possible. Over the ensuing months ARRL staff were involved in writing a series of polygon optimisation programs which would improve the rendering quality and "fly-through" speed of models ported onto SuperVision. These were applied to the Trent 800 model successfully. Additional routines were written to colour code individual pipe routes selectively and to segment pipes into groups of objects, thereby allowing their removal and manipulation.

Before Rolls-Royce's entry into ARRL's VRS Initiative, the final stage in the feasibility project's history was to port the Trent model onto a more powerful platform – the Silicon Graphics RealityEngine – to investigate model rendering (texturing and anti-aliasing are dedicated hardware functions on the SG machine, thus providing the professional image quality required in a project of this sort). This work now continues using the Onyx RealityEngine2 System.

7.7 VR and advanced microscopy

Another important line of research, which is attracting serious interest across the continent, relates to the field of nanotechnology and visualisation of materials and objects at a microscopic level. Scanning tunnelling microscopy (STM), developed in 1981 by Binnig and Rohrer at IBM's Zurich research labs, is a relatively recent development in surface analysis. The technology uses a piezo-electronic probe to mechanically scan a surface, generating topographical information down to Angstrom levels. Since its output is in the form of pure height data, STM has relied from its inception on computer visualisation to generate understandable visual images. However, until recently, these highly complex images have typically taken several minutes to render on the STMs' host workstation. Now, through the advent of powerful, hardware rendering systems (such as the Silicon Graphics platforms mentioned above), it has become possible to produce these images in fractions of a second, making real-time, first-person interaction possible. These possibilities led to a collaboration between ARRL and the University of Salford's Microscopy group, under Dr. Steven Donnelly, to demonstrate how VR techniques could enhance the data visualisation, and perhaps generate a whole new interface for the group's STM, which was designed and built entirely in-house. The current workstation-based user interface and visualisation system had been developed for the STM group by members of the ARRL's Human Factors team, so this was used as a starting block for the further work investigating immersion. The first stage of work, to generate meaningful surface displays on a VR system, was achieved in early 1992, but the speed of interaction was inhibited by the performance of available computing platforms. With ARRL's acquisition, through VRS, of an SG Onyx platform this year, the project was reactivated. The graphics performance of the Onyx was judged suitable for the complexity of the surface geometry, generating a comfortable 30Hz for medium to high complexity images of around 40k polygons. The current work involves using multiple STM scans at differing levels of magnification to generate an automatic level of detail management. When the user flies towards a surface feature of interest, the STM re-scans that region at higher resolution, and inserts this data into the surrounding lower detail topography. Users can then scale themselves down, effectively to "zoom in" on this new detail, or increase their virtual "size" to traverse large areas quickly, balancing resolution against area of interest to keep a fast, smooth frame rate.

The next stage in the work is to use a special fast-scanning STM. WA Technology of Cambridge has offered to build a system which could scan complete data sets every 10th of a second. This higher speed would allow real-time image acquisition as well as visualisation, effectively closing the control loop, changing the application from one of visualisation and control to one of telepresence or, perhaps more suitably, "nanopresence". Further functionality will be added to the system, courtesy of a new STM probe, again developed in-house, which will permit the use of surface lithography techniques. This new nanomanipulation system will allow the user to manipulate and reposition individual or groups of atoms, opening the way to achieve interactive microengineering. The new STM probe and electronics should come on-line early in 1994, with subsequent immersion demonstrations occurring shortly thereafter.

The immersive interface for microscopy demonstrated its usefulness almost from its first demonstration over a year ago, when surface scientists were able to examine their data in a radically new way (ARRL was the first in the world to demonstrate a VR-STM link). Work continues to enhance system functionality, utilising such peripherals as the Teletact tactile feedback system to simulate surface roughness and texture, until the whole surface microscopy process can be controlled using an intuitive immersive interface.

7.8 Conclusions

Readers can take heart that the "child's game" attitude to VR and associated technologies is disappearing fast. VRS has demonstrated that industry now wants to be involved in VR – over a matter of a few months it has gained credibility, at least from a non-immersive standpoint. It is the authors' opinion that, with technical improvements gaining pace, it will not be long before full immersion for selected applications will also become the accepted norm. Hopefully, with national and international central funding cutbacks, VRS will not be the first and last initiative of its sort in Europe. Only through exposing industries throughout the continent to the potential of virtual reality will the field expand into a technologically acceptable means of designing and implementing human-systems interfaces in years to come.

References

AUKS92   Aukstakalnis, S. (1992), Silicon Mirage: The Art and Science of Virtual Reality. Open House (Seattle, USA).

DONN93   Donnelly, S.E., Connell, A.P., et al. (1993), A Scanning Tunnelling Microscope for the Study of Surfaces Irradiated with Low Energy Ions; Journal of Vacuum Sciences and Technology; March/April, 1993.

EARN93   Earnshaw, R., M. Gigante and H Jones (Eds., 1993), Virtual Reality Systems. Academic Press.

KALA93   Kalawsky, R. (1993), The Science of Virtual Reality. Addison-Wesley.

PIME92   Pimental, K. and K. Teixeira (1992), Virtual Reality: Through the New Looking Glass. Intel/Windcrest/McGraw-Hill.

THOM93   Thompson, J. (Ed. 1993), VR R&D: A Directory of Research Projects. Meckler, London.

Chapter 8

Applications of virtual reality in training simulation

P. Jackson

It appears that in many ways the current research and development in virtual reality (VR) is being driven by the low-cost entertainment industry, with little appreciation of the requirements of a 'professional' user. Such restrictions as poor visual resolution and frame-rate, long processing latency and unusable interfaces are not acceptable in most modern training systems.

This chapter will introduce some of the issues involved in specifying and meeting the requirements of today's training simulation systems, and attempt to identify where the 'new technology' of VR fits into the domain of training simulation. It will conclude with a look at some of the training domains in which VR appears to offer most potential over existing systems.

8.1   Introduction

Training simulation can be defined as 'an artificial device or environment which represents a real situation in such a way that a positive transfer of training can be achieved outside the real situation'.

This represents a very wide domain, from cardboard cut-out models to complex military full mission flight simulators. For the purposes of this chapter, I will limit myself to training devices based on computers running simulation software.

Today's customer recognises the cost effectiveness of using computer-based simulation for many areas of training, but is also very conscious of its limitations. For example many of the fundamental fighting conditions for dismounted infantry (cold, wet, fatigue, fear, stress) are still most effectively trained 'in the field'.

The customer is also becoming increasingly aware of the importance of matching the training equipment to the training requirement, derived from the rigorous application of training needs analysis and human factor disciplines. The training equipment may well consist of a suite of graduated training devices, where the student progresses, for example, from a self-paced desktop computer based training (CBT) system through more complex part-task trainers (PTT) to multiple networked full mission simulators (FMS).

This chapter will provide some insight into these and related issues, and then discuss how current and future virtual reality technology can be applied to training simulation.

8.2   What are the requirements ?

8.2.1   Introduction

It is not my intention to set down facts and figures for various types of training simulator, but rather to give some idea of how we approach the task of defining the requirements and also introduce some of the other engineering disciplines applied in today's industry to ensure that the customer receives an effective training system for minimum life-cycle cost.

8.2.2   Who is the customer?

There are many examples of large engineering programmes suffering schedule slippages; often one of the quoted reasons being that the customer has changed the specification. Another common situation is that a system is delivered which meets the specification, but is then found to be partially or totally unusable – this has been equally true in the training simulation industry in the past.

One of the principle reasons for these situations can be that in fact the wrong 'customer' has been identified and satisfied – in the final analysis the customer must be the one that has to use the equipment to obtain transfer of training.

To illustrate how this situation might arise, take for example a training simulator for a new UK military aircraft. We, the training system contractor, receive a specification of requirements from the appropriate department of the MOD(PE). It is tempting to believe that the MOD(PE) is the customer since it is their name on all the documents.

However, the MOD(PE) in turn have their customer who is the head of the appropriate section of the Royal Air Force who will receive and use the training equipment, say a group leader. The specification for requirements may have been generated by his staff, in consultation with various other departments. But remember that they may be experts but will not be the users!

At the end of the day the users are the instructors and the trainee crew who use the training simulators to train and be trained. So are these the true customers to approach when interpreting the requirements?

The sting in the tail is that military personnel are moved around posts at regular intervals, thus the users that you identify and interview when interpreting the requirements will probably not be the people who will test, accept and use the equipment when it is delivered in 2–3 years time.

It is realistic to accept that some of the detail of the requirements may change over the procurement period. In the end the onus tends to lie with the supplier of the training equipment to attempt to design and deliver a system capable of coping with these and similar situations with minimal cost and schedule impact.

Perhaps the lowest risk approach to the specification and design of such equipment is to impartially apply well defined professional disciplines as much as possible. This may not result in equipment that is any one individual's ideal, but it will stand the best chance of being acceptable to all.

The next few sections will introduce some of these disciplines, and indicate where and how they can be most advantageously applied.

8.2.3 Training needs analysis

Training needs analysis (TNA) provides a systematic method for analysing a training requirement and specifying the functional requirements for the training equipment. Once a system is designed, its effectiveness in meeting the training requirement can be evaluated.

It is desirable that simulation fidelity and capability is sufficient to ensure the required transfer of training, but not to grossly exceed it since this would generally increase system cost with no return. Another area to which TNA can contribute is that of the instructional facilities, identifying what monitoring and trainee performance assessment facilities are required.

Where it is inevitable that engineering trade-offs must be made between technical complexity (i.e. cost) and training benefit, TNA techniques can provide a quantitative 'figure of merit' against each training requirement.

This systematic approach to TNA identifies and prioritises required simulation cues for each mission or training task, then determines to what fidelity each can be created in a given system. This will also assist in defining what type of training device can best be used, e.g. CBT, PTT, FMS.

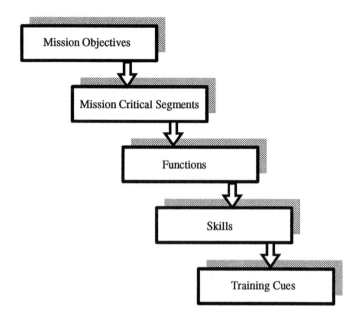

Figure 8.1   *A typical TNA sequence*

The following top-down classification is typical of a military aircraft TNA – the 'mission' can represent any training requirement (see Figure 8.1).

(i)   Define mission objectives. This can be 'fast jet interdiction/strike' for example

(ii)   Identify mission critical segments. These will include briefing, take-off, re-fuel, ingress, strike, egress, landing etc.

(iii) Identify functions. Against each mission segment, identify and analyse the functions, e.g. engine control, flying control, observation, weapon selection etc. Rate according to criticality

(iv)   Identify skills. Associated with each mission critical function will be the skill type, e.g perceptual, cognitive, psychomotor or procedural

(v)   Define required cue fidelity. The cues required for each mission critical function can be estimated from observation and careful interviews with skilled subject matter experts (SMEs).

Most training situations will require elements of all four skill categories. Take for example training a pilot: Initial pilot instruction will include 'cognitive' teaching, with the accumulation of understanding of aerodynamics, engines, systems, navigation, meteorology etc. The pilot also has to learn procedural skills such as dealing with an engine fire, weapon selection and activation etc.

Then there are the psychomotor skills such as the use of the controls to fly straight and level, co-ordinated turns, take-off and landing. Finally, in order to perform the mission they will need perceptual skills, including observation of the out-the-window visual scene, IR (infra-red) and radar sensor imagery etc. together with the mental 'data fusion' of all the inputs in order to compile and update his mental model of the environment.

So the result of this systematic analysis will be a specification of the cues required and their minimum fidelity in order to achieve the required transfer of training. The system can now be designed to meet these requirements and, where technologically problematic or costly, an engineering trade-off can be made with full awareness of its impact on training effectiveness.

8.2.4 *Human factors*

The considerations of human factors have a very high profile in all modern military systems, not just training simulators. As an example consider the requirements for MANPRINT which is mostly unknown outside defence circles but is probably the most comprehensive approach to human factors currently applied [MANP].

MANPRINT stands for manpower and personnel integration in system acquisition, and is a defence procurement programme aiming to enhance human performance and reliability in the operation, maintenance and use of manned systems, including ergonomics and safety issues as well as the training, numbers and skills issues. It originated in the US army, and is steadily spreading throughout NATO.

MANPRINT considers the following six 'domains':

- manpower – the demand for human resources in terms of numbers

- personnel – the manpower in terms of trade, skill levels and physical attributes

- training – the process which prepares personnel to do their jobs to particular performance standards

- human engineering – improving performance or eliminating sources of error through system design

- system safety – identifying and measuring safety hazards, to maximise operational readiness and performance through accident prevention and minimise safety retrofits

- health hazard assessment – preserve and protect the health of the users and enhance user performance and system effectiveness.

As the result of systematically considering the implications of human factors in these domains, the equipment can be developed, delivered and used, with a high degree of confidence as to its acceptability to all persons involved with its everyday operation.

8.2.5   Integrated logistic support

This is an area of rapidly growing application within military programmes, being concerned with defining a logistic support strategy and, by performing a logistic support analysis (LSA), defining what tasks are required to be performed throughout the life-cycle of the equipment to keep it operating at the optimum level.

Operational and logistic support can be one of the major life-cycle costs of a large system, but is highly dependent on system reliability and maintainability, which in turn depends on the design and technology employed.

Integrated logistic support (ILS) is a management and technical process through which supportability and support considerations can be integrated into the design early in the life-cycle of a project. It represents a comprehensive, structured and disciplined approach to designing for supportability and the management of total support.

By applying ILS systematically throughout the design process the customer can be made confident that predictions of life-cycle costs are based on sound information and design practice.

8.2.6   Models, databases and courseware

Perhaps one of the most significant features of a good training simulator, and one that is apparently sometimes overlooked by many newcomers to training simulation, is the quality of the simulation models, databases and courseware.

Software models and/or tabulated performance data for the primary components in a simulated vehicle or system can be acquired (often with great difficulty) from the appropriate manufacturer. Unfortunately many models are not suitable for deterministically real-time 'man-in-the-loop' simulation, and must be modified or re-engineered.

Environmental databases, including terrain and bathymetric profiles, features (point, linear and areal), 2D and 3D models etc. can be difficult to transform for simulation use, despite the increasing availability of digitised data. In order to obtain the best results within the limited capacity of visual image generators with such capabilities as level of detail (LOD) switching, the modelling process becomes a highly skilled art.

Courseware generation and verification can be extremely time consuming, especially if some degree of 'self-instruction' capability is required. It may also be necessary to produce extensive 'briefing' material in order to introduce the trainee to the training situation and present them with preparatory information.

8.2.7 Summary

For many customers the purchase of training simulation equipment is a large capital outlay and a vital component of a larger programme, thus they will wish to be reassured about the capability and costs of the equipment and services they are purchasing. The professional application of the above disciplines will go a long way towards this.

Not all of the above factors need be considered in exhaustive depth for every small training system, but the customer is becoming much more 'canny' both in military and civil training system procurement.

You will note that I have said nothing about good design processes and methods, quality assurance etc., I presume that these are generally accepted concepts today and should need little further discussion here.

For many applications it should not be forgotten that a major part of the cost is the preparation of the software models, databases and course material – this investment must be weighed against the temptation to invest in very low cost inadequate hardware.

8.3   The training environment

8.3.1 The new technology

Let us explore where the 'new technologies' of VR fit into the training simulation domain. By any measure, some of us in the training simulation industry have been 'in virtual reality' for the last fifty years, and I am afraid that generally we are not getting too excited by all the media hype! Fully immersive simulation, interactive environmental models, tactile and haptic feedback, three-dimensional sound etc. are all standard on any advanced training simulator.

That is not to say that developments in VR are being ignored, but we are perhaps better placed than many to perceive their pros and cons. The fundamental requirements of a 'manned' training simulator have been derived over years of painstaking research, and it can be quite distressing to see so much work re-inventing the wheel.

As I commented earlier, training simulation covers a very wide range of equipment categories from the very simple to the highly complex. I will paint 'past/present/future' pictures to indicate how I see the trend from 'hard' (i.e. hardware based) to 'soft' (i.e. software based) training devices.

8.3.2   A set of co-ordinates

Zeltzer [ZELT90, ZELT92] proposed an interesting set of co-ordinates within which to place virtual environment simulation systems. They propose that three orthogonal axes of a unit cube represent verity, integration and interface. Thurman and Mattoon explored this further [THUR91] (see Figure 8.2).

'Verity' is used here to define a scale ranging from simulating the physical world as we know it, to simulating a totally invented world. For many training simulators we are situated towards the 'real world' end of the scale, with the 'invented world' most useful for entertainment and some research domains.

'Integration' is used to define to what degree the user is involved in the virtual environment, ranging from not at all to totally integrated. Not integrated corresponds to computer batch processing, whereas totally integrated corresponds to total immersion.

'Interface' denotes the scale of 'naturalism' of the human computer interface. At the 'artificial' end of this scale come keyboards, mice etc., while at the 'totally natural' end the user is not aware of any interface at all.

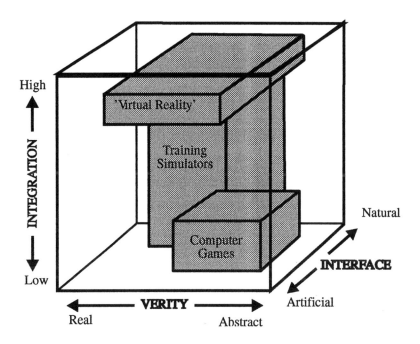

Figure 8.2 *Co-ordinates of reality*

8.3.3 Fidelity

Of the above three axes, the one most at issue in human training is that of 'verity', or fidelity as it is more commonly termed. Fidelity can be defined as a combination of accuracy (i.e. truthfulness) and realism, the most desirous mix being determined by the training application [BARN91].

Referring again to the skill categories identified above, the essential requirement for cognitive and procedural training is accuracy, in that information given must not be suspect. There is less emphasis on realism, indeed it may be advantageous from a training transfer aspect to remove distracting 'realistic' features. It may even be advantageous to actively distort the reality in order to better demonstrate the subject matter.

For psychomotor and perception skills the user requires realism above all else; most flight simulators primarily fall into this category with the cockpit furnishings and controls, visual, motion and aural cues, and the response of the vehicle and its systems all intended to convey the user into a sense of 'being in the real thing'. That is not to say that it is inaccurate – much effort and cost is spent on ensuring that databases correspond closely with the real world.

Accuracy is fairly readily defined, and where inaccuracies do exist the training material can be planned accordingly to cope. Realism is rather more difficult to measure, being fairly subjective. It appears not to be linear in nature, but rather reaches a sufficient level at which a step 'suspension of belief' occurs. Unfortunately the point at which this occurs differs from person to person – children are very susceptible but military combat pilots are generally less so.

8.3.4   Negative training

Perhaps one of the most often heard phrases in training simulation is 'negative training', which is where, usually due to some deficiency in the simulation model or ancillary hardware, the trainee receives training which is not as it is in the real world.

This is undesirable, and in many cases can be dangerous when the trainee returns to the real world. A basic example would be incorrectly modelling aircraft performance such that a trainee gets used to flying lower than he can safely do in the real aircraft – the first time he flies for real he kills himself.

The usual approach is that negative training is never acceptable in training simulation, but it is being recognised that in some non-critical areas some degree of negative training can be allowable provided it can be rapidly re-trained out when the trainee returns to the real world. Again training needs analysis is essential to determine where this is the case, and where the cost savings are justified.

Consequently it is conceivable that the current low-fidelity VR technologies could be used in certain situations, provided that provision is made to ensure that any negative training is immediately re-trained out.

8.3.5   A developing interface

8.3.5.1 Training past
In the past, before computer based training simulators (and in the present where training simulators are not available or suitable), the trainee would either learn on the job or in a special training 'real' environment.

Take, for example, infantry in small arms training; the trainee would fire real bullets from real rifles at real targets – though presumably cutouts rather than living humans.

And that is the major drawback of such systems – the environments are relatively fixed, especially the terrain profile, and the dynamics are fairly constrained in their capabilities. Safety issues lead to severe restrictions on what can be done, especially with live rounds.

8.3.5.2 Training present
At present levels of training simulation technology, the equipment with which the trainee physically interacts will still be real hardware (or a high fidelity replica), with the remainder of the environment 'beyond arm's reach' being simulated.

So our infantry trainee will be firing a replica rifle (perhaps a production rifle modified with a compressed air recoil device, a laser aim-pointer and various other sensors) at a totally computer generated environmental (visual) scene. Since the environment is 'soft' the trainee can now learn how to handle his weapon effectively in a much more realistic and dynamic scenario.

There is still the limitation, however, that in order to train with a new weapon type, the simulator specific hardware will need to be designed and manufactured and perhaps new operating models and interface software developed.

8.3.5.3 Training future
With the incorporation of sufficiently high fidelity interface hardware of the VR type, the 'soft' environment is brought closer to the trainee's person. Basically everything outside of his skin may now be modelled in software.

So our infantry trainee, wearing his full fitting force / haptic feedback exoskeleton with high resolution head-mounted visual, can now run through the scenario, throw himself to the ground behind cover and fire whatever weapon he has been issued with. Of course, wading through swamps and operating after being inflicted with non-fatal injuries might still pose problems of safety and fidelity.

8.3.5.4 Training sometime
But don't stop there! Who needs interface hardware?

Taking the logical development to the next stage in order to overcome the limitations of the previous one, we might perhaps get inside the trainee's periphery and interact directly with his nervous system. All his environmental interactions, both input and output, could be direct to the brain, thus all senses could be simulated (not now stimulated) to a high level of fidelity, and all muscle signals would be intercepted by the simulator to control the model of the trainee in the environment.

Maybe not next year, but who is to say never.

8.3.6   Summary

Coming back to where we are today then, the way I look at VR is that it promises to provide for 'generic human interface hardware' which brings the 'soft' environment within arms reach and ultimately as close to the user's 'periphery' (skin) as possible.

Naturally the software modelling of the immediate environment requires the development of new techniques in order to provide sufficiently high fidelity interactions, but it is only a conceptual progression beyond what is done already.

Vision has the highest bandwidth input to the human body, and it is the one most understood in traditional training simulation technology. Head-mounted displays have been researched in several simulation systems and, although very expensive, have been demonstrated to have no insuperable problems. Basically despite technological advances it still costs large amounts of money to provide high fidelity visual imagery; once this is accepted the problem more or less goes away.

I believe that the main constraint to applying VR in training simulation is the lack of high fidelity generic tactile/force feedback. This would have to be capable of 'full suit' scale in order to meet the requirements of many training systems. Unfortunately I see no way of avoiding the 'exoskeleton' concept whereby the limbs are encased in a mass of linkages and actuators.

Only then can we simulate the major part of the environment generically without special to task mechanical 'props', which from my viewpoint move us no great distance from where we are now. Again it could be argued that the problem could be readily solved with the application of enough money and some serious engineering – I don't believe there are many fundamental physical problems inherent.

8.4   Applications of VR to training simulation

8.4.1   Remaining constraints

As can be seen from my discussion above, I perceive that the objective of VR techniques should be to totally envelop the trainee in a generic, synthetic, software generated environment capable of effective application across a wide scope of training domains.

However, it still would not be possible to sit back and say "we can do anything now – its all in software!", without considering the implications of the very significant remaining constraints on the interface. These include:

- the very real physical existence of the remaining hardware, including the head-mounted visual system, the 'exoskeleton', trailing umbilicals etc.

- other senses not stimulated – sense of heat, smell, taste

- ambient environment – air movement, pressure, temperature, fluids

- Rotation/gravitation/acceleration/vibration forces – can use existing motion systems

If no reliable high fidelity tactile/force system is available (and it is difficult to consider any of the current range of 'data gloves/data suits' as high-fidelity or reliable), this constraint list extends significantly:

- only very constrained hand and limb movements possible

- mostly need non-generic hardware to support specific training

- little (and/or unrealistic) tactile or force sensations

And if we limit ourselves to a 360x240 pixel LCD HMD, all we can mostly do is train someone to use low-fidelity VR equipment – and then only for the limited time that the average person can stand 'experiencing' the VR environment.

8.4.2 Unsuitable training domains

So let us consider which training domains the 'software-closer-to-the-skin' approach may not be suitable for. Consider the following, if nothing else from the safety angle:

- donning and operating in protective clothes (e.g. NBC gear)

- direct contact with fluids (e.g. underwater swimming)

- the application of sheer physical strength (e.g. construction industry)

- interacting with own body (e.g. inserting a contact lens)

- rapid and large scale movement (e.g. many sports)

- very close contact with another person or persons (e.g. wrestling)

- 'violent' physical operations (e.g. hammer and nail)

- team operations where close interaction is necessary (e.g. civil pilot/copilot)

Without high fidelity tactile/force feedback equipment the vast majority of training requirements will not be met unless extensive use of special to task hardware is used, which is not within my definition of generic VR.

8.4.3 Suitable training domains

Let us consider which domains current and 'near future' VR will be suitable for. Despite the negative approach of some of the preceding sections, there are undoubtedly an enormous number of potential application areas.

The following factors would assist in the application of current VR:

- where people operate equipment in isolation from other people, or by communication through voice etc.

- where restrictive equipment (suits and helmets) is worn in the real world

- where the real world environment is already VR based

- where the training session can be brief, i.e. before the onset of 'virtual (real?) sickness'

- applications where the real world can usefully be scaled or distorted

This last item is of great interest and can lead to a vast number of possible applications. By scaling linear dimensions the trainee can 'manually' build molecules or move mountains. By scaling physical constants the trainee can learn to perform complex activities, for example by reducing gravity it is much easier to learn to juggle.

Theasby [THEA92] gives an overview of the various categories of 'traditional' training simulation equipment and where VR can perhaps be applied. One of the most immediate applications will probably be in 'next-generation CBT', where the trainee is generally performing cognitive/procedural training and current VR technology can usefully enhance the trainee's involvement.

8.4.4 Non real-world training

Although I earlier defined training simulators as being concerned with real world situations, note that many concepts which cannot normally be experienced in the real-world can be taught by computer simulation. There is some overlap with research simulation, but I briefly suggest the following as an initial stimulus:

- experiencing and teaching mathematical concepts (e.g. curved space)
- teaching 'invisible' activities (e.g fluid dynamics)

8.5   Conclusion

This chapter has presented some of the issues which must be addressed when defining the requirements for a training simulator, and has then explored where the emerging technologies of 'virtual reality' fit within the domain of training simulation.

It has been indicated that much work has been performed over the years in evolving disciplines for professionally defining training simulator requirements, and that, from one viewpoint, the virtual reality technologies are a natural progression from existing simulation equipment and not the fundamental leap that many tend to believe.

References

BARN91   A.G.Barnes 'The Compromise Between Accuracy and Realism in Flight Simulation', AIAA, 1991

THEA92   Theasby,P.J. 'Virtual Reality & Simulation', Meckler VR '92.

THUR91   R.A.Thurman, J.S.Mattoon 'Virtual Reality: Theoretical and Practical Implications', I/ITSC, 1991

ZELT90   Zeltzer,D. 'Virtual Environments: Where are we going?', IDATE, 1990

ZELT92   Zeltzer,D. 'Autonomy, Interaction and Presence', Presence, 1992

MANP   MoD MANPRINT Office: AD JS 33 (HF, Training and Simulation)

Chapter 9

Low-cost virtual reality

R. Gallery and B. Gibson

A topic in innovative computer systems, virtual reality is an endeavour to occupy human sensory systems to such an extent that participants become immersed in an artificial environment detached from the world around them. The man/machine interface techniques emphasise natural and intuitive control and response. They have relevance to forthcoming multimedia interactive systems, in particular compact disc-interactive (CD-I) where the acceptability and success of application programs depends upon naturalness and ease of use. At PRL a head-mounted, position sensing, wide field colour stereoscopic display has been built that, together with real time 3D image synthesis capability, allows the potential of these concepts to be evaluated. Application software that illustrates the techniques of virtual reality has been written and includes a virtual art gallery and an entertainment game. We have shown that a CD-I player equipped with an additional digital signal processor board could be a realistic low cost platform for the 3D image synthesis software that is required.

9.1 Introduction

Virtual reality is the concept of replacing human sensory interaction in the natural world with interaction in artificially generated environments. The concepts embodied are far from being new; whenever people look at pictures they are partially replacing real world input by artificially created visual input. Advances in computers and their peripherals now allow a far stronger sense of involvement in artificial worlds to be attained. Visual display systems that are capable of presenting moving stereoscopic colour images that cover a substantial proportion of the eyes' visual field are becoming possible. Sensors that measure head, body and limb position are available and may be configured to convey human commands and intention to a suitable computer system.

The reasons for working on virtual reality are not solely to achieve immersion in artificial environments, perhaps more importantly, the man/machine interface issues involved allow for a more natural and powerful control of systems over a wide range of application areas. A person wearing a glove equipped with sensors for finger and hand positions is able to convey intention and exercise control of a system in an intuitive and easily learnt manner. Using a head-mounted visual display equipped with a head position sensor, computer applications requiring navigation information as input may be routed intuitively by head movements, with immediate visual feedback to the displays confirming and reinforcing the direction in which a user is looking.

At PRL the incentive for investigating virtual reality arises from our expertise with advanced computer graphics systems and a need to establish the potential of the techniques for future interactive systems, with particular emphasis on low-cost solutions for consumer applications. With consumer applications, amongst the issues are whether innovative control mechanisms are beneficial to certain classes of application software titles, and whether new application opportunities will arise by fully embracing the ideas of virtual reality. These ideas may find application in any of the main title areas covering entertainment, education and information.

In this article we will review some of the equipment and techniques that are associated with virtual reality, then go on to describe some applications that have been designed to illustrate the potential of these ideas.

9.2   Virtual reality practitioner's toolkit

To become immersed in a virtual world, a prime requirement is a display system that substitutes normal visual input to the eyes from the world around with display images from an artificial source, usually a computer graphics engine or television input. It is essential that the display image covers ideally all, or a substantial proportion of, the total human visual field. There have been two approaches to attaining this display ideal. Manufacturers of aircraft simulators for the aerospace industries use expensive large multiple-projection displays that cover the whole effective visual field. This approach is tractable because the view from a cockpit seldom requires total uninterrupted 360° vision. The alternative, far lower cost approach, that we and many others have adopted, is to place small displays close to the eyes, fixed relative to the head, that subtend a large angle to the eyes. With this arrangement a user sees only images on the displays, all other visual input from the real world is hidden. A sensor fixed to the head measures the direction in which a user is looking, this measurement is used to determine the image sent to the displays by an image controlling computer. As a person looks around, so the images they see move in unison, giving the visual allusion of looking around the world.

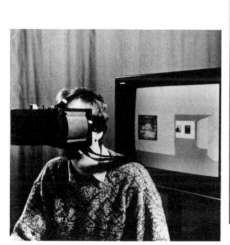

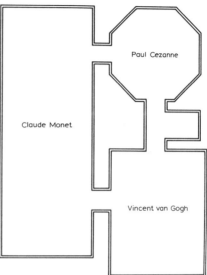

Figure 9.1 *Helmet display system* **Figure 9.2** *Plan of virtual art gallery*

A stereoscopic head-mounted display system has been constructed using colour liquid crystal display (LCD) television panels, converging lenses and mirrors to give a low weight assembly that a has a wide visual field (Figure 9.1). As far as possible the helmet was constructed with off the shelf components, to minimise design and construction costs. Critical design constraints were the resolution of available LCD panels and a need to minimise the mass and moment exerted by the head assembly. LCD panels of 75 mm diagonal with 384 x 264 pixels are viewed using 42mm diameter lenses of 150mm focal length, giving an optimum compromise between screen pixel structure appearance and angle of view. The optical path is taken through 90° with mirrors so that the panels are mounted to give an interocular separation of 60mm and to minimise vertical downward moment. The system gives realistic wide angle, well converged stereoscopic images with a pixel structure visible without being too obtrusive. Attached to the head mount is a magnetic sensor that forms part of a proprietary system [POLH] that remotely measures azimuth, elevation and roll. It also measures spatial position in three dimensions.

Some of the peripherals required for virtual reality work are already being manufactured for commercial sale, indeed SEGA are reported to be bringing out a £200 head-mounted display later this year. Also available are sensor gloves and even complete sensor suits. A low cost glove is the Power Glove from Nintendo Inc [MATT89] which sells for about $50 and was aimed at the computer games market. So far no equivalent low cost data suit has emerged (existing early versions cost many thousands of pounds).

Central to a virtual reality system is a graphics images processor. We have targeted our work towards real time 3D image synthesis in which images of real world objects are synthesised from defining data structures. The consequence of this is that realistic looking scenes in which the viewpoint and viewangle are variable quantities may be generated from comparatively simple data sets. The downside is that the computations required to generate images that respond almost instantly to requests for changed view points (implying a new image synthesis rate in excess of 10Hz) require high performance software and hardware. To meet these requirements two different hardware configurations have been used. One consists of a Sun workstation with the addition of customer designed hardware specific to 3D image calculations. This platform is used for the gallery virtual reality application described below. A second approach has been to use standard CD-I players with the addition of an experimental digital signal processor (DSP) board fitted in the expansion board slot, illustrating what may be achieved with low cost systems. This platform is used for the shooting virtual reality entertainment game described later in this chapter.

9.3   Applications of virtual reality

Our aim is to illustrate some of the powerful advantages that virtual reality gives to interactive visual applications. In this first example, virtual reality is used to show a virtual visit to an art gallery (Figure 9.2). A user wearing a head mount is able to look around gallery rooms hung with paintings and adorned with sculptures by the worlds' greatest artists. As a visitor's head moves and turns, the image processing system outputs to the displays images which are appropriate to the position and eyesight direction within the gallery (Figure 9.3). Look to the left or right as desired and so the pictures and view seen change. Look upwards to the ceiling and the fresco comes into view. Move forward a little to get a closer look and inspect the detail, move backwards to get an overall view. All this happens completely naturally as users move their heads, and their bodies move within a range of a few feet. "Look over there! I'd like to move through that corridor into another room".

Figure 9.3   *Art gallery. Looking around Vincent van Gogh room with views through to Paul Cezanne room*

At this point our technology has some limitations, the magnetic sensor operates over a range of a few feet and the virtual distance is some tens of feet. Our solution is to use a different interface device for walking about the gallery. This is a proprietary interface device consisting of a sprung ball that detects forward, backwards and sideways forces exerted by the hand and outputs appropriate movement signals [DIME]. It also detects a twisting action indicating a turning request. Using this device we complement the head-mount sensor signals and have a satisfactory and natural strategy for our visit to the art gallery. Moving around, it becomes apparent that movement through the walls or to walk through the sculptures is impossible, just as we'd expect of the real world. Want to know more about a particular picture? Then look at it and press a button that initiates a recorded sound segment giving some interesting background information. For our demonstration, the gallery consists of three principal rooms hung with paintings by Cezanne, Monet and van Gogh, with sculptures by mainly lesser known artists. The size of the gallery, its number of rooms and pictures, could be extended without detriment to application performance.

The apparent structure of the gallery, the walls and ceilings, and the contents, have been created by the well known computer graphics technique of polygon modelling. The defining data structures consist of the cartesian co-ordinates of polygon vertices, a polygon descriptor, and the surface rendering applied to these planar polygons. Polygon rendering definitions use either a uniform surface colour data descriptor that is concise, or a two-dimensional full colour data array (texture map). Realistic images are created from this data by the graphics processor, taking into account viewpoint information from the virtual reality viewing helmet. In the gallery the pictures that adorn the walls are derived from texture maps. As modelling sophistication and realism increases, so does the size of the defining data set, which increases the computational load on the graphics processor and slows down the display update rate. This would seem to suggest that the larger the gallery in terms of number of rooms, the slower the performance. In practice it is possible to segment the data into separate rooms so that only data for the current room being viewed are processed, making application performance largely independent of gallery extent.

We have illustrated a particular gallery hung with paintings by a selection of artists, the attraction of virtual reality is that on another occasion we could mount an exhibition by different artists or visit an entirely different gallery just by changes to the application data. Related application areas are numerous; visit museums, cathedrals, castles or wander through your dream house and suggest modifications before a brick is laid! Using, in addition, a sensor glove you may pick up virtual objects to inspect more closely, or move your hands to perhaps indicate some preferred option.

The natural navigation and exploration that is a feature of virtual reality may be extended to the retrieval and access of information on databases. Such concepts as the virtual filing cabinet are a possibility.

Entertainment and games are areas where virtual reality is expected to become popular. Manufacturers of arcade machines are already demonstrating equipment that adds heightened realism to the popular applications such as driving and flight simulators. Competitive games using more than one participant fighting battles or overcoming challenges in a virtual world have also been demonstrated.

Figure 9.4   *Sequnce from shooting game showing landscape, bird acquisition in gunsight, and target hit*

To illustrate the potential of virtual reality in an entertainment context, a simple shooting game has been designed. The application uses 3D graphics image synthesis, and the graphics kernel is capable of rendering about one thousand polygons per second, sufficient to give real-time operation to a carefully designed application. By using two players where the operation is synchronised it has been possible to generate images from slightly different viewpoints and so create fully stereoscopic images with the virtual reality helmet.

Wearing a helmet, a participant is placed within a countryside scene, able to look around in any direction and make limited movement in the terrain by walking about (Figure 9.4). Superimposed upon the display is a gunsight crosshair giving the impression of aiming a shotgun. Looking around and surveying the landscape, game birds fly about at random. The user attempts to align a bird with the crosshairs and fires shots using player mouse buttons as a trigger. Upon a direct hit there is an explosion and the bird falls to earth. A shot that goes close but nevertheless misses aggravates the bird which flies aggressively towards its assailant. To add interest, a scorecard visible on the display records the difference between the number of kills and near misses. Involvement with the action is heightened by the use of appropriate sound segments for shots being fired, explosions and angry birds.

An interactive kitchen design package [PULM89] produced to illustrate the advantages of real time 3D image synthesis has been adapted to run on CD-I players. View direction and position within a synthesised kitchen is currently controlled with the assistance of a mouse and view cone displayed over a 2D kitchen plan. Adapting this application to virtual reality would allow a user to move and look around the kitchen in a more natural manner.

9.4   Conclusion

Our work on virtual reality has concentrated on the construction of a realistic head-mounted wide field stereoscopic display system with position sensors and the design application software to evaluate its potential. Associated with virtual reality are also novel interface devices such as hand position sensing gloves and body position sensing suits.

It is clear that a virtual reality helmet has powerful advantages in interactive applications that require navigation and exploration. So intuitive and natural is the interface that new users are immediately able to move around a virtual environment. These advantages are applicable over a wide range of interactive applications. In addition to being an excellent navigation interface, a virtual reality helmet (through its exclusion of extraneous visual input and its wide view) gives a heightened involvement with applications. This is particularly relevant to interactive applications produced for the games and entertainment sectors.

9.5   Acknowledgements

We gratefully acknowledge the extensive contributions of David Penna and Paul Winser to the work that has been described. Thanks also to David Atkinson who was responsible for mechanical design of the helmet display system.

References

POLM   Polhemus, P O box 560 Colchester. VT 05446 USA

MATT89   Mattel Inc 1989 Hawthorne CA 90250 USA

DIME   Dimension 6 control device, CIS Graphik & Bldverarbeitung GmbH Postfach 100180 D-4060 Viersen 1 West Germany

PULM89   Plummer M and Penna D E Mass Market Applications for Real Time 3D Graphics, Computer Graphics Forum Vol 8 No.2. pp143–150 1989

Chapter 10

Intelligent life in a virtual world

I. Andrew and S. Ellis

Many VR development systems enable the user to create three-dimensional worlds, colour, alter and then explore them. At this stage, the virtual world itself is static and the environment is lifeless; there are no moving objects and no scope for interactivity other than moving the user's viewpoint. The world is dead.

However, many applications demand more from the virtual world and an advanced VR development system can bring life to these simulated environments. Thus, objects within a virtual environment can be assigned dynamic attributes and even artificial intelligence. Their characteristics and reactions to various stimuli will mirror movements and activity in the real world. Intelligent virtual worlds are vibrant, dynamic and alive.

The first programming language specifically designed to control object behaviour in a virtual world is called SCL (Superscape Control Language). This provides the functionality and flexibility to control simultaneous parallel object activity within a virtual world.

10.1 Virtual world types

Virtual reality is a powerful tool for modelling situations in the real world, or making abstract data seem more real. In both cases, realism can be greatly enhanced by giving motion and complex behaviour to objects.

When classed according to movement and control, virtual worlds fall into four basic categories.

The first are the static computer-generated worlds produced by architectural CAD programs fall squarely into this category. They may be real time walk-throughs, but there is no interaction; the world is effectively dead.

The second contains worlds with movement. Most systems provide some form of motion control on objects, from simple dynamics to full simulation of the physical properties of the object in question. Each object reacts in a manner consistent with a set of rules – the laws of physics for that world. This is crucial as a first step towards interactivity. If the user collides with a ball in the virtual world, he would expect the ball to be affected in some way. Using a basic laws-of-physics interaction model, the expected reaction would be for the ball to move, bouncing off intervening objects, and eventually coming to rest. Extended laws of physics are used in this kind of system for molecular modelling, for example.

The third area is behavioural control. Objects can detect circumstances arising in the virtual world, and respond to them in a variety of pre-programmed ways. This can effectively override the laws of physics for the world. Push a car and it will roll in a straight line until stopped. A car with complex behaviour can be made to turn, accelerate and decelerate under its own initiative, or make choices about its route depending on the state and position of other objects in the virtual world.

The fourth area is the so far unrealised goal of true artificial intelligence of objects.

10.2 Applications of behavioural control

The advantages of behavioural control go a lot further than merely providing playthings for the users of largely static virtual worlds. The VR system can be used to visualise inherently complex dynamic processes, such as the movement of parts through a factory, dynamics of smoke particles and other fluids, or for modelling human behaviour.

With dynamic interaction between the user and the virtual world, useful work can be accomplished in a virtual environment. Visualisation of real world events can be accomplished, and actions taken depending on their nature. The objects in the world can be programmed to provide important visual and aural cues for situations requiring immediate attention and also for potentially disastrous courses of action.

Many companies are already using behavioural control in their virtual worlds to simulate complex situations for training purposes, effectively using VR systems as low cost simulators.

The Advanced Robotics Research Laboratory (ARRL) at Nottingham has several industrial robots. These devices are heavy duty and can cause considerable damage if handled incorrectly. By modelling the behaviour of the robot in a virtual world, inexperienced users can be trained in its use without danger to themselves or others. The virtual robot can be programmed by the trainee to accomplish certain tasks in the same way as the real machine.

British Telecom at Martlesham have demonstrated a prototype application using VR for monitoring network integrity and fault finding (see Figure 10.1). Each node in a large multi-tier network is programmed to route messages around the system, and can be made to fail either randomly or at a signal from the user. The software will then redirect the messages to avoid the failed node, just as in the real system. The eventual aim is to use the system as a front end for remote debugging of the network and recovery of the failed nodes. The behaviour built into each node is far beyond a basic laws-of-physics interaction model.

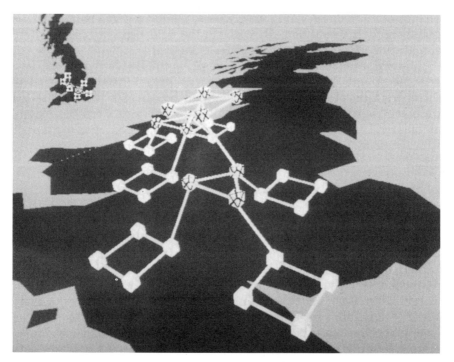

Figure 10.1   *British Telecom network modeller*

One particularly striking example of behaviour modelling is VEGAS (Virtual EGress Analysis System), developed by G. Keith Still of Colt International to model the way that large numbers of humans behave in emergencies such as a fire. Up to 200 objects each have one of a set of different rules for getting out of buildings. Some will go straight for the exits, others will attempt to stay with their "children", even if it means going back towards the source of danger, and some may be given the limitations experienced by handicapped people.

Once set up, the simulation is then run and viewed in real time, with the user controlling the viewpoint and any additional hazards that may occur. By modelling a variety of simple behavioural responses to the virtual environment, the actions of a crowd can be predicted with a fair degree of accuracy.

More traditional simulation is being used in military applications for training the operators of guided missile systems. The application is a significant step up from the previous system being used, which involved laser projection of dots of light to denote the target and missile positions. The new system models the flight of the missile according to the inputs it receives from the trainee, and presents views of both it and the target in a much more realistic way. This gives the trainee a much better feel for situations that would actually occur in the field, especially effects like obscuration of the missile by its own smoke trail.

A final, completely different, example is the BBC's Cyberzone programme, where teams of contestants run their virtual counterparts through a maze of puzzles and obstacles. Although a few of the obstacles were controlled by a remote user, all of the puzzles were completely automatic. The behaviour of each puzzle was pre-programmed to interact with the user and react to given responses.

10.3 SCL – An object control language

All these examples run on desktop PCs using the Superscape VRT, and the various behaviours are therefore modelled using the Superscape Control Language (SCL). This is a language whose syntax is based on C, with a heavy bias towards virtual world manipulation. Object status and relationships can be interrogated, and any attribute of the object modified in real time. Each object may have its own SCL program, effectively running in parallel with those on the other objects. This allows complex emergent behaviour to be modelled very easily if a large number of similar units is required.

Each type of object can be programmed as a single entity and then duplicated as required. Each SCL program can refer to its own object, allowing the program to be duplicated with the object and still retain its correct context.

SCL is a powerful language with over 500 built in commands, which is compiled to intermediate code for speed and space reasons. The source code for SCL is not stored with the objects, or indeed at all; only the user's comments and variable names are stored directly. When edited, the source code is decompiled from the intermediate compiled code and the comments and names reintroduced. This ensures a compact final code which is not dependant on any particular machine or processor.

```
resume(0,1);
if(activate(me,0))
{
    repeat(10)
    {
        moveby(0,100,0,me);
        waitf;
    }
    repeat(10)
    {
        moveby(0,-100,0,me);
        waitf;
    }
}
```

Figure 10.2 *Example of SCL code. Object will 'jump' when activated by user*

SCL is a co-operative multitasking language. Every frame, each object in the world executes its program in turn, handing over to the next at convenient points. Objects may take as little or as much time as is necessary to complete their task. This eliminates a lot of the headaches in trying to debug many parallel threads in a pre-emptive system (one in which the execution overseer suspends and resumes execution of the programs at arbitrary times). By resuming the SCL program each frame from where it left off, a program may effectively take several frames to complete (see Figure 10.2).

10.4 The future

A lot of research is going on in the various fields of artificial intelligence, and it is reasonable to expect that this will influence the future direction of behavioural control in virtual worlds.

Evolutionary growth of behaviour patterns is one of the most interesting of these areas. Bryan Salt, one of the researchers at Dimension International, has built a model of a simple self-evolving ecosystem consisting of bees and flowers (see Figure 10.3). Successful bees are the ones that are attracted to the flowers; successful flowers attract the bees. Additional factors influence the bees' choice of flowers, when to breed, how much time is spent foraging and how much looking for a mate, and so on. The descendants of both bees and flowers differ slightly from their parents, allowing natural selection to take place. All this is modelled using SCL.

Figure 10.3   *Bees and flowers evolution demonstration*

By allowing complex behaviours to "grow", rather than building them, much more complex interactions can be developed in less time. The evolutionary process supplies the intelligence, rather than having to rely on the programming skill of the virtual world designer. The utility of this approach will continue to grow as more research is done.

10.5 Conclusion

The inclusion of behaviour control in virtual environments is an important part of making them realistic, interesting and useful.

The concept of a separate control language for object behaviour is an important alternative to the traditional method of building the behaviour into the object code of a VR application. When this is coupled with a Graphical User Interface, the resulting combination can be extremely powerful.

Chapter 11

Applied virtual reality

P. du Pont

11.1 What is virtual reality?

Virtual reality is a set of computer technologies which, when combined, provide an interface to the computer with which the user can believe he or she is actually in a computer-generated world. This computer-generated world might be a model of a real-world object such as a house that has not yet been built, an engineering model of a factory or a product under design, or it might be an abstract world which does not exist in the real sense, such as a chemical molecule, a representation of fluid flow-lines in a CFD model, or even a 3D representation of a multi-dimensional financial dataset.

The computer interface provided by virtual reality is very three-dimensional. The world or model to be viewed by the user is apparently real, completely surrounding the user, and responds appropriately to the user's natural motion and interactions. The user is fooled into believing that the model being viewed is real – and a deep and accurate understanding of the model is thus obtained.

Two key concepts of virtual reality are immersion and interaction. The user must feel immersed in the virtual environment, and must be able to interact with the world using hands, arms, head, legs etc. Without both immersion and interaction, the user will not readily believe that the world is real, and will not gain the same depth of understanding of the model or data.

11.1.1 User benefits

What are the principal benefits of virtual reality? The benefits can be lumped into three areas: understanding, experiencing and learning. In all cases, virtual reality is providing a view that, to the user, is apparently real, and it is from this that the ultimate benefits are derived.

Figure 11.1   *Simulation of Early-stage theatre design*

Understanding
When there is a three-dimensional object or relationship to be understood, virtual reality brings clear benefit. If two piece-parts have to be designed to interrelate, virtual reality (VR) can allow the user to see prototype designs of these parts as full-sized or larger (relative to the user), solid, three-dimensional objects. They can be manipulated together or apart by the user with his hands, in much the same way as he might pick up a 3D puzzle and examine it with hands and eyes.

Seeing objects as full-size is one very important benefit of the extra understanding virtual reality can bring. Looking at a computer-generated photograph of the facade of a building is not nearly as beneficial as standing on street level and looking up at the three storey building with the building properly placed in its context. The VR view wins hands down every time.

Experiencing
Being able to have convincing experiences is another benefit of virtual reality. Whether these are for entertainment purposes, or to properly appreciate a situation that you may someday be faced with, VR lets you experience a situation or environment with a high degree of realism.

The simplest proof of the value of VR in experiencing things accurately is in airline pilot flight training. Although today's flight simulators pre-date what is now called VR, they are exactly what immersive virtual reality is all about. There is a certain level of stress that is important in training pilots to fly. Flight simulators and immersive VR recreate this situational stress very well, to the point that pilots can take on quite a 'sweat' along with fear of failure.

Learning
Finally, many applications of virtual reality can be lumped under the heading of learning, or training. The benefit that VR brings by faithfully re-creating a situation is valuable training to the user, presumably at a much-reduced cost.

Take an example from the military training scenario. Every shoulder-mounted anti-tank missile fired in practice costs hundreds or thousands of dollars. Using virtual reality, there is a fixed up-front cost, and virtually no per-session consumable cost. The key is to accurately reproduce the training scenario. That's what virtual reality is all about.

Consider the layout and operation of a complex control room, maybe for a power plant or ship. By building the control room first in virtual reality and then testing it out with real users, the designers will gain tremendous information about the suitability of the layout and ease of use. Furthermore, trainee operators can familiarise themselves with the layout, and even practice operational situations, all in a virtual environment. Multi-user VR systems enhance this by allowing for the training of whole teams of operators.

All of the benefits that VR brings to understanding, experiencing and learning, derive from the immersive and interactive capabilities that virtual reality brings the user. Without immersion and interaction, VR is no more than the high-quality graphics already available today.

11.1.2 Technical overview

How is virtual reality achieved by computer? There are a number major activities that the computer must perform:

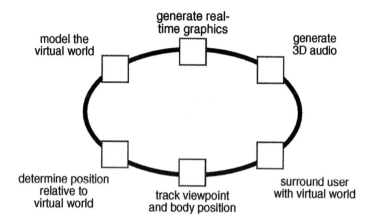

Figure 11.2   *Major activities performed on the computing platform*

Generate real-time graphics
If the user is to see the virtual world, the computer must generate 30 frames per second of images of the world. This is so that, as the user moves his head, walks or reaches out and picks up an object, the images drawn by the computer quickly and accurately reflect what the user is doing and his new view of the world.

Generate three-dimensional audio
Similarly, the sounds heard by the user must be real and accurate. This includes the three-dimensional spatialisation of the sounds, the inclusion of reflections and echoes, and the Doppler effects heard with moving sounds or moving listeners. It should be remembered that, while graphics are commonly considered to be the critical element necessary for good virtual reality, the human ears are much more important for understanding a real-world three-dimensional volume, and any virtual reality capability will be incomplete if the world is not full of the appropriate sounds, however small and insignificant they may appear to be. Furthermore, full binaural, spatialised audio is necessary to match the characteristics of real-world sound.

Surround the user with the virtual world
This is usually achieved today by wearing an immersive headset, and within a few years this will be replaced with a simple visor and ultimately eyeglasses. In any case, small television screens are suspended in front of the eyes, and earphones are placed in each ear. The result is that wherever the user moves to or however he turns, the virtual image is always displayed around him.

Track user's viewpoint and hand position

For the computer to know what image to generate on the headset, there must be some form of tracking of the positions of the head and hands of the user. This often takes the form of a very simple magnetic field source, with several magnetic sensors placed on the user – typically one on the head and one on each hand.

Determine user's position relative to objects in world

Given 3D position tracking of the user, the computer must then compare this position with each and every object in the virtual world. This allows the computer to show the virtual objects in the correct position relative to the user, and to determine when the user has touched any virtual object.

Model the virtual world

Finally, the computer must maintain an accurate model of the virtual world. These models often start with today's three-dimensional computer-aided design (CAD) packages, but they must be enhanced to provide additional information necessary to the virtual world but not included in the CAD package. Examples of such additional information include animation, sound, reactive properties (when the user touches the objects), motion constraints etc.

Each of these is critical to the success and value of the virtual reality. All must operate simultaneously and in tandem, combining into a single virtual world that is alive and acts and reacts appropriately.

Division Limited believe all of these tasks can most effectively be accomplished on a distributed computing platform, so that individual tasks can operate in parallel on a separate processor when necessary. For instance, real-time rendering is most effectively done on a processor which is optimised to keep a graphics pipeline full. Tracker interrupts, collision detection, or generation of audio waveforms will detract heavily from the graphics performance if the processor is shared.

Equally importantly, the distributed platform may span several different hosts, which may be physically separated. If you are running in a Silicon Graphics environment, you might use your Crimson RealityEngine2 for rendering, while off-loading the tracking tasks to an Indigo connected via TCP/IP. Multi-user simulations (in which two or many users share and interoperate in the same virtual environment) must use two or more machines. With dVS, the inter-user communications are at a fairly high level, so they can happen effectively across a standard network.

The virtual reality application development cycle is illustrated in Figure 11.3 (overleaf).

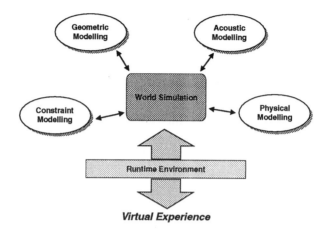

Figure 11.3   *VR application development cycle*

Software systems are available to help the applications developer integrate virtual reality with existing and new applications. Division Limited's dVS VR operating system provides a layered approach which is clean and simple, requiring a minimum of attention to the VR systems side of the development cycle. Further, it effectively hides a distributed software and hardware environment from the developer.

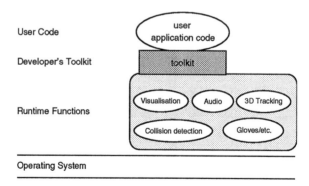

Figure 11.4   *dVS layered development approach*

To further simplify the user's work, and to remove the requirement for any programming, Division Limited has developed dVISE which allows the importing, assembly and specification of VR-properties for objects designed in existing CAD packages. Using dVISE, a complete virtual environment can be quickly built, from within the virtual environment. Thus, starting with a basic building geometry, the user can walk around in the virtual simulation, placing tables and chairs, defining door pivots, assigning audio properties, recording animations by tracing them with their hand in 3D-space etc.

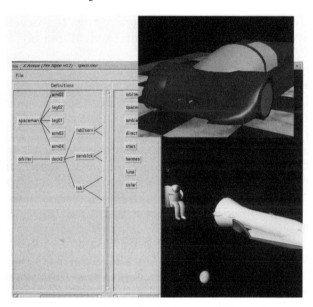

Figure 11.5   *Using dVISE in both 2D and 3D modes*

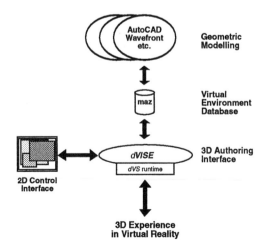

Figure 11.6   *The dVISE authoring system block diagram*

11.2 Application examples

11.2.1 Computational chemistry

In conjunction with the University of York, Division Limited, IBM (UK) and Glaxo Group Research are collaborating on the development of virtual reality tools for molecular modelling and, ultimately, for rational drug design.

Existing molecular graphics systems allow the scientist to interact with and manipulate a representation of a molecule in an attempt to understand and model the relationship between the three-dimensional structure and the function and properties of the molecule.

Virtual reality makes this activity much more intuitive for the molecular chemist: instead of trying to understand what is clearly a three-dimensional problem on a two-dimensional screen with a two-dimensional mouse, the chemist can hold the molecules in his hands, twist them, turn them, see how their shapes relate, understand the different energy levels represented by different positions – as if the molecules were real, solid objects.

For example, when two molecules are brought together, or when a complex protein chain is twisted to a new shape, particular atoms within the structure repel other atoms as they move into close proximity. The Glaxo system can show this steric hindrance in real time, by representing the changing resistance of atoms by changing colours. As the hindrance is computed in real-time as the relative position of the atoms changes, the chemist gets an immediate feedback and, using his natural eye-hand co-ordination, he can adjust the position and shape appropriately.

Figure 11.7   *Interactive molecule manipulation during drug design*
Courtesy of G. Tomkinson & Glaxo Group Research

11.2.2 Complex lighting visualisation

Thorn EMI's central research laboratories use virtual reality to visualise lighting designs. Proposed architectural designs and lighting fixture layouts are modelled with a radiosity-based lighting algorithm. Both flat-screen and immersive views are obtained and, again and again, the immersive views have given a much deeper and clearer understanding of the design. The designer fully appreciates the critical nuances, while the customer or client can be placed directly in the design to communicate its features and benefits.

In one example, Thorn created two identical rooms connected by a doorway. In one room, the lights were mounted directly against the ceiling, while in the other, the lights are suspended by cables. Looking at a 2D perspective screen shot, the rooms look very much the same. However, using the VR system, stand in one and walk into the other, and the difference in spaciousness becomes immediately apparent. Sit down in a real chair (located where the VR chair is) and stand up in the virtual room with low-hanging lights, and your reflex action will be to duck your head. This is the nuance VR makes apparent.

Figure 11.8 *Concept design of lighting in office*
Courtesy of Thorn EMI CRL

11.2.3 Kitchen showroom sales

One of the most visible virtual reality successes world-wide has been Matsushita's kitchen design project. The goal has been to produce a system suitable for use in kitchen showrooms that can let customers see their new kitchen before they buy it. Customers bring a floor plan of their existing kitchen to the showroom, where they specify the new units they wish to buy, including colours, product type, layout etc. The design is quickly assembled into a VR model, and the customer is placed right in the kitchen.

This concept has also been applied in other areas. One of Division Limited's customers is using virtual reality to sell landscape designs, by putting the customer right into the landscape and letting them walk around as if it were real. We have seen several examples of customers who have shown virtual reality models of new buildings. In one case, 40 not-yet-built houses on a new housing estate were sold by virtual reality simulations!

11.2.4 Living environment simulation

The Living Environmental Systems Laboratory (LEL) at Matsushita Electric Industrial Co. has developed a system for simulating complete living environments in virtual reality. The goal of this fully immersive application is to provide building designers with an accurate simulation of the air conditioning, lighting and acoustic characteristics of a room or building under design.

Figure 11.9   *Interactive visualisation of CFD airflow data*
Courtesy of Matsushita Living Environment Labs

There is a growing demand for detailed simulations to improve the overall environmental amenity of a building. In the past, this has been done by building full-scale mock-ups, and testing the actual air conditioning units, lighting fixtures and furniture layout. This has proved costly, time-consuming and inflexible, and is a limiting factor in designing better building environments.

By using virtual reality, LEL can experience and interact with the simulation of the room. A detailed simulation, including airflow and temperature distribution (using a computational fluid dynamics model), sound levels and lighting levels (using radiosity algorithms), are run in advance on a supercomputer. The resulting data are overlaid on a geometry of the room, with fixtures such as walls, windows, tables, air-conditioning units, speakers etc.

The user can then walk around the room (in the virtual environment) and see the data levels at any point. For instance, by holding out his hand, airflow streamers shoot out from the hand showing where the air flows from that point, and what the temperature distribution is like. Or, the user can drag a semi-transparent sheet (or plane) across the room, and watch a colourful contour map dynamically change as the cross-section is dragged through the volume of the room.

The result is a quantitative evaluation of the room environment, as perceived by the human. And as the user is actually in the virtual room, he can walk around and understand all aspects of the environment, from any position in the room.

11.2.5 Industrial concept design

Turning to the automotive engineering field, students at the Coventry University School of Art & Design are using virtual reality to visualise their automotive designs in full size and in a natural context long before mock-ups and scale models are built. The goal is ultimately to do away with many of the concept design models which are built at great expense during the life of a vehicle design, while eliminating design flaws much earlier in the design process.

Looking at a photograph, even a large one projected on a wall, doesn't give the same information as standing next to a car and walking around it. Watching the specular reflections on the hood move as you move or watching the car drive by on a street gives you a better understanding of the form of a car than just a photo.

Equally important, being able to open the doors and the boot, both to check the articulated function and to see the new appearance, are actions you can only perform in virtual reality. And a new level of design-formanufacturability or maintenance is possible when you can guide a virtual hoist to place your engine under the hood of a vehicle under design.

This work can be extended beyond cars – it applies equally well to trains, aeroplanes, even manufacturing plants under design.

Figure 11.10 *Walking around a concept design of a car in a showroom*

11.2.6 Office furniture in context

You have all experienced the change over the last twenty years from individually-assigned enclosed offices to open-plan work areas in which individuals sit within their own half-height partitions. One of the world's largest office furniture manufacturers is using virtual reality to simulate the complete open-plan office. The challenge is to design furniture that is attractive, fits with the open-plan concept, maximises privacy, minimises office noise and is pleasing to view.

11.2.7 Astronaut training

In the Netherlands, TNO-FEL have been studying virtual reality for training astronauts for manoeuvring during space walks. The difficulties of zero gravity are compounded by bulky space suits, and virtual reality makes a perfect simulation tool to re-create this experience.

Consider two examples: first, as there is no gravity to give a natural orientation and no ground for stability, simple acts such as moving are difficult. If the astronaut tries to push a heavy beam away, he will actually impart the motion on himself rather than the beam.

Second, when using jet propulsion system, astronauts find they can easily project themselves well beyond their target, or impart a rotational motion on themselves. This is because there is no friction from the atmosphere or the ground to constrain motion. Even for simple motions, vector mathematics must be considered, and careful planning of any action is necessary.

Using a VR simulation system that properly models motion in space, the trainee can practice working under these conditions. Even with only ten or fifteen minutes in the system, the user quickly gains a new appreciation of how to manoeuvre.

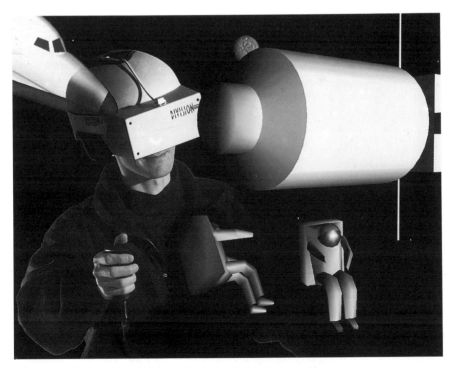

Figure 11.11 *Simulation of astronaut space walk*

TNO's space walk system allows two users to train simultaneously, for example to co-ordinate the joint assembly of a space experiment. Again, the dynamics of two people working in space are challenging to master, and a device such as this provides a very realistic simulation of motion in weightlessness and in a vacuum.

One lesson has been learned from this simulator: three-dimensional audio could be of great value in helping astronauts to communicate in space. Since space suits do not have rotating helmets, and therefore the astronaut cannot turn his head around to view behind him, there is a difficulty of identifying where other astronauts are located. 3D audio was found to be invaluable when simulated radio communications were spatialised, as the ears can identify where the sound is coming from when the source is out of sight.

11.2.8 Stinger missile training

TNO-FEL have also developed a prototype virtual environment-based trainer for Stinger portable air defence missile systems. The trainee receives a full simulation, in which they are there, standing in an apparently real landscape, with realistic targets, activities and trainee interaction. They can practice operating procedures, target identification and acquisition and missile firing, without the complexity of the traditional dome display system.

Figure 11.12 *Training infantrymen to operate shoulder-mounted missiles. Photo courtesy of TNO-FEL*

11.2.9 Marketing drugs to doctors

An international drug company is looking at virtual reality in a totally different context: as an aid to selling their products to doctors. The function of a particular drug is complex to explain; using virtual reality, the doctor can manipulate a model of the drug and understand its function from an interior view.

Here VR is used to play back a three-dimensional script of action and reaction, between molecules representing critical portions of the dangerous virus, for instance, and the drug designed to destroy it. The doctor sees a clear representation of how the drug works at the molecular level, and the drug company gains a marketing tool that effectively explains a difficult concept.

Furthermore, as the doctor can play an interactive role in the simulation, for instance by selecting which site to bond at or changing the position and shape of the drug, their learning experience is enhanced.

11.3 Conclusion

In short, virtual reality allows you to be somewhere or to experience something, that you cannot easily experience. Maybe the building doesn't exist (VR in architecture) or the event is expensive to reproduce (VR in training) or a model is complex and hard to visualise (VR in abstract data modelling). Virtual reality can give you the experience at a minimum of cost and with a high degree of realism.

Chapter 12

VR in a service company

T. Howe

12.1 Introduction

Science fiction or the ultimate computer interface? Virtual reality (VR) could either be heading for the cul-de-sac of promising technologies which never made it, or on the road to creating major social change. Some believe that VR has the potential to transform all aspects of our lives.

It is clear that VR has much to offer. It can transport a user into a completely synthetic three-dimensional environment which offers varying degrees of visual, haptic and audio feedback. Current applications suggest uses and benefits never possible with a two-dimensional interface.

But where could this vision and promise take today's companies? This chapter will look at a service company which depends heavily on information and technological advantage for success. It will describe the key elements of the business and then try to identify where VR could be put to work. This will be followed by personal observations of how the VR industry could improve its chances of commercial success.

VR is a tool which could transform a mass of data into a wealth of information. Its strengths lie in presenting a three-dimensional world and letting the user wander freely through it, interacting with and manipulating the entities which reside in that world. Most design and multi-dimensional data related work will benefit from the use of VR. But it could offer a great deal more.

VR offers opportunities for transforming communications and personal interaction. Perhaps the easiest and most extensive current communication channel is Internet ("the net"). Many thousands of commercial organisations, academic institutions, research laboratories and individuals are in some way linked to Internet, freely communicating with each other irrespective of physical ability, location, time of day etc. Individuals across the world can communicate with each other simply by leaving messages in each others "mail boxes". Information can be transferred and applications accessed on any number of computers all linked via Internet. Currently constrained by interaction through a keyboard, imagine being able to step through the screen and enter a VR communications environment. It will be possible to hear, see and touch your thoughts.

Individuals have the freedom to change when they use electronic communication. Their actual "real" persona can be left behind. When they start typing they can assume a different character. A normally timid person could assume an assertive or even an aggressive mode of communicating. People are free to shrug off the cloak of day-to-day reality and assume an alternative character free of the restrictions of face-to-face communication, talking, moving and looking like anyone they chose. How many Margaret Thatchers or Harrison Fords might meet each other in a VR communication environment?

Another area of promise for VR is training and development. The commercial world uses a wide range of technologies to improve the effectiveness and productivity of its employees, e.g. computer based training and interactive video. VR applied to the fields of counselling, stress management, role play and personal development has great potential. Any company interested in the well being of its employees offers at least one of the above services. There have already been promising experiments using VR as the medium for child patient counselling and phobia counselling. These medical applications could easily be transferred to industrial training and development.

Although we do not yet have intelligent computer generated "actors" a person may enter a VR environment and take on the persona of another individual. The look of the VR persona is obviously computer generated but the voice can also be altered to reflect a different character. With the "tutor" taking an assumed role with a computer generated character and the "trainee" interacting with the VR tutor the possibilities are endless.

12.2 The physiology of a service company

This chapter aims to describe a structured approach that can be used to identify potential applications of VR in a service company. The first step of the approach is to model what the service company actually does. There are any number of techniques and methodologies that could be applied. The particular technique chosen has been successfully used in a service company by the author.

Logical process modelling is a technique which provides a hierarchical view of a company's key business activities, it ignores existing methods, organisation and technology, i.e. 'What its does' not 'how it does it'. It is an approach that allows separation of business processes from any influence of existing organisation or technology.

A logical process model can help identify where VR can be successfully applied. The model allows us to:

a.   view the key processes and how they relate

b.   map the features of VR against those processes

c.   identify possible opportunities to apply VR in each process

By mapping possible applications of VR onto the model in this way, it is possible to then build an overall strategy for implementation. The high level model for the service company looks like this:

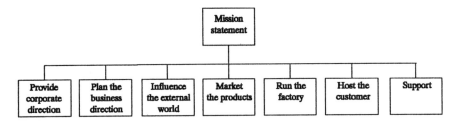

Figure 12.1   Top level process model

The seven key processes in the model are all required to support the mission statement. This model comes from a transport company. The model of a financial services company or a catering company for example would be slightly different. The complete model would extend to perhaps five or six layers below the level shown in Figure 12.1 and have upwards of 100–150 processes. It is very detailed and, if done correctly, i.e. not reflecting existing technology or organisation, is a useful tool to examine possible future uses of VR in the service company of the future. Each leg of the model is further sub-divided and contains the processes shown in Figure 12.2.

The model has given us a logical, structured and hopefully exhaustive check-list against which we can start mapping VR onto the business. By identifying the strengths and weaknesses of VR, taking into account its potential availability and limitations, we should be able to start mapping out possible applications.

Provide Corporate Direction
This would include formulating and communicating the strategy of the company. Defining and evaluating possible alternatives. Designing the organisation to deliver the strategy

Plan the Business Direction
Understanding the markets. Developing new products. Planning the operation to deliver the strategy

Influence the External World
Promoting the business image. Forging personal contacts. Building business relationships

Market the Products
Informing the market. Providing the means to sell products. Concluding contracts. Maximising product contribution

Run the Factory
Delivering resources. Managing the tactical operation. Providing tactical support

Host the Customer
Customer service both before, during and after delivery of the main product

Support
This area contains all the support type processes such as: recruitment, staff development, purchasing, accommodation, systems, and cash management

Figure 12.2   *Lower levels of the process model*

12.3 The strengths and weaknesses of VR

Before we start to map VR onto the business we need to examine what VR can do today, what it might do tomorrow and what its limitations and boundaries may be. Will it add value to the business process? Each business application will have its own specification, its own demands on speed, resolution and realism, and with VR you get what you pay for.

The growing VR industry offers a vast array of solutions. It is possible today to buy a "desktop" VR application for less than £15,000. At the other extreme it is possible to spend literally millions of pounds and obtain photographic realism and the very latest in full body tracking devices. The question at the end of the day must always be, will it *add value* to the bottom line?

VR offers the chance to step through the two-dimensional interface we are restricted to today. VR offers the chance to become part of our synthetic three-dimensional creations. Many of today's businesses need to understand and manipulate a mass of data to make decisions. "What-if?" "How would it look if?" "What's the bottom line?" and "What does all this really mean?" can be heard in offices across the world. Two- and three-dimensional graphical representation of data has provided the means to quickly assimilate information and help find the answer to some of these questions.

The ability to move around and examine from all angles a graphical construction of data will provide another level of understanding. However, to provide this facility for a simple accounting spreadsheet would be like using a sledgehammer to crack a nut. But for a flight scheduler controlling the financial yield of twenty flights a day each carrying 150 passengers paying 25 different fares across a time frame of 300 days or a bond dealer trying to understand the movement of 500 stocks across three markets, virtual reality has much to offer.

The facility to "be there" and see for yourself cannot be replaced, or can it? For product designers the ability to present their designs on a flat two-dimensional medium cannot replace the real thing. The ability to move around the design and view it from all angles is difficult to reproduce artificially. Any designer has to make a cognitive leap from what is seen in two dimensions to what it actually could look like in reality. Even seeing a sophisticated computer image is no stand-in for actually being there. Virtual reality could be the tool to remove the need for designers to make the cognitive jump.

Alternatively, "being there" can be a problem for individuals wanting to practice some kind of interpersonal skill with another individual. It would be extremely risky telling an angry customer "I am a trainee. Could I try the broken record assertiveness technique on you?". Any individual developing their personal effectiveness or customer contact skills needs a non-threatening environment in which to practice. Existing solutions include the use of CD and laser technology to reproduce "scripts" of various situations. The most commonly used method however is still role-playing with other individuals and trainers. Technology would need to move forward a pace before VR could offer a cost effective, acceptable replacement for this area but experiments with facial waldos and animated characters have proven the potential in this field.

The combination of high quality graphics, immersive headsets and video will provide the opportunity for individuals to take part in and acclimatise to situations which would otherwise be a unique or at the very least a rare occurrence. In the way that the flight simulators of today provide pilots with the opportunity to experience and train for the unexpected, the extreme and the stressful so VR could provide doctors and nurses with the experience of extreme situations, e.g. multiple pile-ups or large explosions. It is assumed medical staff are used to this type of experience but even they can find such situations shocking, very stressful and difficult to cope with.

The typical St. Johns first aid courses need no longer be constrained to using slides of industrial accidents. Participants could experience them in full immersive 3D. Market makers can perhaps experience the sheer panic of a collapse in the stock market. Customer contact staff could experience (in safety) the pandemonium when customers find out their flight has been delayed for yet another 12 hours. All these situations happen in reality but because they happen rarely nobody has the chance to practice or feel what the experience is really like. Taking part in a VR simulation could give individuals the chance to react more effectively if they ever have to experience the real situation.

Another strength of VR as with other computer simulation is the ability to repeat an event time after time, not only from beginning to end but jumping to particular points or events. Running through an event, task or activity in slow motion is also possible. Teaching presentation skills, juggling, a delicate heart operation or ticket collectors the task of controlling a platform, the ability to control and manipulate the environment in which the "trainee" is operating could be invaluable.

One last strength of VR is the ability to put you where you could not possibly be, to allow you to do the "impossible". Air traffic controllers will one day be able to "fly" around their control zone, seeing each of their charges in their correct position in three dimensions. Potentially dangerous situations will be highlighted and communications will be initiated by a point and click style routine, but the pressure of making a cognitive interpretation from two to three dimensions will be eliminated.

Transport planners and analysts will fly a graphical representation of their business, able to interrogate the yield or seat factor of a particular coach, train or plane. By flying down the route, interpretations of area or time based revenue could be made possible. The presentation of a business in this way will facilitate easier understanding of the business, its performance and its key drivers.

Geologists and geophysicists will have the facility to bore down through solid rock and then abruptly turn and follow a particular strata, not only making the interpretation of seismic and other surveys easier but also reducing the cost of searching for minerals and hydrocarbons. Doctors and surgeons already have the ability to view the progress of their endoscope. An immersive VR solution would provide them with a much safer means of navigating what could potentially be a damaging piece of equipment around a delicate human body. The ability to move around a three-dimensional world and to actually feel you are part of it, to have personal presence, is a facility which many industries and professions would prize.

To briefly summarise the strengths and weaknesses of VR we can turn to a classic business tool, the SWOT analysis (strengths, weaknesses, opportunities and threats). The discipline of the technique is to record only those qualities which are unique to VR, it can sometimes lead to a very short analysis but one which will focus our attempts to apply VR to our service company.

Strengths (real, unique strengths)
*   The ability to transport an individual to a virtual environment and, by replacing any or all of an individuals sensory input with synthesised reproductions, convince an individual of his/her presence in that environment.

*   The ability to present an environment of three-dimensional constructs and entities which can be influenced and manipulated by participant(s) in the same environment

Weaknesses
*   The current dependence on bulky hardware for some sensory interfaces, i.e. tactile, force and visual feedback

*   The current cost versus performance versus realism compromise

Opportunities
*   The need for businesses to gather and control data to maintain their operations and develop new opportunities and markets etc. will provide a pull for solutions that can help investment

*   The pressure to reduce costs and reduce the time it takes for a product to get to market will provide a pull for solutions that can simulate real products

Threats
*   The tendency for the popular press to over expose a germinating industry could increase expectations beyond the means to deliver

*   This in turn could have a negative effect on possible future investors making them cynical, wary and averse to even minor risk

12.4 How could VR help a service company

We have a model of a generic service company and we now have a clearer understanding of what VR offers. We now need to map one on to the other. This produces a two-dimensional matrix mapping the bottom line processes of our company against the strengths of VR, where those strengths could add value to that process. We can then use alternative dimensions to produce judgements concerning the potential benefit, time scales and likelihood of each application. To present a complete matrix is beyond the scope of this chapter. The following paragraphs summarise a possible matrix taking each high level process individually.

12.4.1 Provide corporate direction

This process, more than most, needs to assimilate and interpret a mass of textual data and intelligence. Existing tools include databases and perhaps in limited areas hypertext. The appearance of VR would certainly provide a means to visualise and organise the mass into a comprehensible, usable resource. New techniques of graphical presentation and storage of large textual databases are currently being researched and look promising.

However, in today's company the reality of where this work is done could limit the opportunities. The departments which are involved in providing corporate direction tend to be relatively conservative, viewed as non-core or non-strategic and consequently short on funds. They are used to dealing with a mass of paperwork which traditionally has not been computerised.

I would propose this area is an unlikely candidate in the commercial application of VR. There will be forward thinking organisations, but this area is likely to be a follower rather than a leader.

12.4.2 Plan the business direction

This area is perhaps one of the potential hot spots for VR activity in the service industry. Activities such as understanding the size of the markets, auditing products, planning schedules, planning resources and developing products could all use VR to help either reduce costs or increase revenue.

The strength of VR to put analysts in the middle of a construction of their market enabling a swift assimilation of a mass of data, to understand a key driver or spot a future trend will, I believe, be one of the entry points of VR into a company.

Developing a schedule or plan needs many iterations at any level. When the plan is for 250 planes to fly between 200 destinations utilising 15,000 flight and cabin crew it is a vast undertaking. Any tool which can help visualise the development and influences of this size of plan would yield large savings. A tool which can help a planner actually see relationships between one plan and another, one resource and another could potentially revolutionise large scale planning.

As previously indicated in this chapter, VR is a tool which can assist the product designer. A service company, like a manufacturing company, has products, although service products tend to be more intangible. The service product, its design and delivery all need to be stringently tested before going to market. Any assistance which can shorten the process can help any company's bottom line. However, this might be an area where the cost/realism/performance compromise would currently rule out VR, but it is still a possible candidate for the future.

12.4.3 Influence the external world

This whole area is about communication both inwards and outwards, i.e. the impact of the external environment on the business and the business impact on the external environment. Businesses must continually gather information and respond appropriately. Current VR technology has nothing to offer this process area. Perhaps in 5–10 years when networked VR will hopefully have established itself in national and international communication infrastructures the technology will add value. Until this happens there is no obvious application.

12.4.4 Market products

Another potential VR hotspot is in persuading potential customers, establishing methods of sale, yield management and focusing sales effort. All these could make use of current VR technology.

We have already seen a certain aftershave being promoted with the use of a virtual glider simulator. Kitchen salesmen in Japan can now use VR as a means to design, quote and sell their products. There is no reason to believe a service company could not use VR as a medium to persuade customers of the quality and value of its services. The only limitation is the headgear and subsequent assimilation period required by a user.

In the good old days when flying was for the limited few, flight bookings were made with chalk on a blackboard in a main booking office. Currently, with millions of passengers flying each year, the complexity and scope requires a very user-unfriendly computer system to be used by thousands of booking agents across the globe. Perhaps VR could bring back the times when booking was conceptually very easy. Might we see the introduction of a VR chalkboard and agents wearing a VR headset?

Yield management is linked to the previous example. Their task is to balance the two conflicting demands of any service company, maximise use of capacity and maximise yield. The two do not naturally sit side by side. By reducing prices any company can sell their full capacity; the trick is to sell the product with the maximum premium the market will take, thus ensuring a profit. Skill in this area means the difference between survival and financial disaster. Unfortunately for the people having to perform this juggling act it usually requires the assimilation of masses of real-time data. A facility which VR has as one of its strengths.

12.4.5 Run the factory

Within the context of a transport company this means delivering resources, managing the actual daily operation, and providing support when required. Apart from the obvious uses for planning and scheduling which I have dealt with, the main use in this area could be for the operational managers, working at the customer interface and dealing with the day-to-day activities.

VR could provide these people with an opportunity to move easily from overseeing the complete operation one minute to zooming down to the minutiae of a particular problem area the next. An airport manager could be "flying" above the airport terminal, seeing where the planes were at a particular time, then seeing where queues were forming at particular desks, then checking the hold up with baggage. With a tweak of a joystick the manager could be communicating directly with a resource manager to arrange resources at a desk or redirecting maintenance personnel to the baggage line. A similar situation could be envisaged for coach, rail or transport companies in fact any company with a large, very active and diverse operation.

12.4.6 Support

This area has perhaps the widest variety of possible VR applications; VR recruitment, aptitude and personality testing could be performed in some cleverly created VR environment. Various areas of feedback, performance reporting, development training and personal effectiveness training could all be possible in VR. Although the technology still has some way to go to catch up with these ideas.

Purchasing and procurement support in a large company needs constant monitoring. Supply lines, stock levels and financial performance could all be the subject of VR modelling. The possible savings in this area could well provide a good business case for introducing VR.

Accommodation can be the biggest dissatisfier in any large corporate concern. VR is already being used to plan office buildings, the office space and to model the responses by the occupiers to various emergency situations to check safety procedures. A good example of this is the design of the Terminal 5 complex at Heathrow airport.

Cash flow is the life blood of any company. No cash in the bank means no funding for today's operation and certainly no investment for the future. Understanding the current financial position of the company is vital for a number of people within a firm. From the treasurer to the accountant. This is sometimes not easy with funds perhaps across the world in any number of currencies and accounts, money committed to paying its debtors and money forecasted to come in from its creditors. All this might be relatively easy for the financial technicians to understand but for others within the company who also need to make decisions based on their understanding it could be the proverbial maze. VR again could provide a tool to help.

Each of these applications will require the appropriate technology to be available at the right price. A business case must be written and approved. Even when implemented, the success or failure of each application will depend on senior management buy-in, level of training, leadership and organisational climate. It is never easy to introduce new technology into a company, the problems increase dramatically when a change of culture or work practice is required. VR will not be accepted into a company because of its current ability to amaze a largely male, relatively young and change-oriented audiences, nor will it succeed or fail purely on its impact on the bottom line. There will be many factors working for and against VR. Success will depend on how well these factors are taken into account and planned for.

12.5 Feedback to potential manufacturers

Having worked in an office environment for longer than I care to mention, there are a number of issues most office workers are aware of. An office can sometimes be a harsh environment for a delicate piece of hardware or a poorly written piece of software. The normal day to day office type activities and the not so normal office terrorist have been the downfall of many a new tool.

The desktop of any information worker is often littered with in-trays, out-trays, files, PCs, cups of coffee and working papers, so much so that many of them find it difficult to find room for a mouse for their PC. The thought of another piece of hardware like a VR helmet to find room for would fill many of them with horror. Many office ceilings these days are "hung" and therefore do not offer a simple, firm suspension. So it would be better to incorporate the headgear into a chair or arrange for it to be neatly and easily stored on top of the PC screen. This would remove another well-known office hazard, loose cables. A cable that retracts into the chair back or desk is a safe cable.

The thought of office workers wandering around a padded cell with a VR headset on does not convince me that this is a technology with a bright future. Information workers will continue to sit at workstations or in small crowded offices or in an even smaller and more crowded study at home. Because of this constraint, the interface for moving around a VR environment needs to be very well designed, compact and usable in a confined area. The software needs to cope with the beginner and the more experienced user. The hardware needs to be simple to use and ergonomically well designed. User friendly visual and sound icons should be used to full effect with the ability to shorten them for the expert.

A relatively minor point perhaps but the success or failure of user acceptance will also depend on the colour and style of the finished products. A boldly designed, black headset that looks like a bird of prey will go down well with certain users but completely turn off others. The thought of sitting in an office with a crash helmet on your head for an hour is not very appealing. Not only will weight be a consideration but so also will air circulation, comfort and temperature.

If you consider the reactions and concerns whenever new technology is introduced, e.g. microwave ovens and possible effects on fertility, keyboards and repetitive strain injury and VDUs affecting the eyes, designers of new technology will need to consider the very real impact of user perceptions. Using appliances attached to the head will be strange and intimidating to most people.

12.6 Conclusions

VR has many potential uses across a service company. The speed and use to which it will be put depends heavily on the development of the technology. Much can be applied today but the real change element of VR will start to have effect when the cost/performance/realism compromise can be achieved without development fees looking like telephone numbers.

I believe virtual reality will slowly find its way into the tool kit of many companies. Initially helping large scale data users but moving into other areas such as training and development and planning. This gradual implementation will require many things from the VR industry. Not least will be user-friendly development tools, end-user tools, well designed and manufactured accessories and simple to assimilate environments.

I have identified many possible applications for virtual reality within a service company. As we begin to understand its impact and implications, new and as yet undreamed of applications will begin to emerge. Could virtual reality change society? change the way companies do business? Many technologies have promised much but failed to deliver. Virtual reality has the promise, time will tell if it can deliver that promise.

References

ASCH92   Asch, T., "Designing Virtual Worlds", AI Expert, August 1992, pg. 23-25.

BENE91   Benedikt, M., "Cyberspace – first steps", MIT Press, 1991.

DAVI93   Davidson, C., "How to make the Mario Brothers smile", New scientist, 13 March 1993, pg. 20.

GEAK93   Geake, E., "Managers struggle to adapt to teleworking", New Scientist, 5th June 1993, pg. 22.

GIBS86   Gibson, W., "Count zero", Grafton, 1986.

HEET92   Heeter, C., "Being there: The subjective experience of presence", Presence, Volume 1, Number 2, Spring 1992, pg. 262-271.

HELS91   Helsel, S. and Roth, J., "Virtual Reality – theory, practice and promise", Meckler, 1991.

INDE93   Index Foundation, HR issues in transformational change, CSC Index, Document 94A, April 1993.

LANI92   Lanier, J., "A brave new world – Virtual Reality today", Virtual Reality Special Report, Virtual Reality Report, 1992, pg. 11–17.

LAQU93   LaQuey, T., and Ryer, J., "The internet companion", Addison-Wesley, 1993.

LATT92   Latta, J., "The business of Cyberspace", Virtual Reality Special Report, Virtual Reality Report, 1992, pg. 27–33.

MEYE   Meyer et al, "Implications for Virtual Reality applications", Presence, Volume 1, Number 2, pg. 185–189.

PIME93   Pimentel, K., and Teixeira, K., "Virtual Reality – through the new looking glass", Windcrest, 1993.

RHEI91   Rheingold, H., "Virtual Reality", Martin Secker & Warburg Ltd., 1991.

SCHN91   Schneider, M., "Virtual Reality – a Reality", Gartner Group Report – T-751-056, 23rd September 1991.

WOOD92   Wooley, B., "Virtual Worlds", Blackwell, 1992.

Chapter 13

Telerobotics in the nuclear industry

W. Webster

13.1 Introduction

13.1.1 Definition of robotics

Robotics has been defined by many people and in many ways. The official robot associations choose to emphasise the programmable nature of the technology, whilst the media and entertainment industries concentrate on the anthropomorphic variants. The Japanese industry considers any non-manual handling device to be a robot and hence include in their surveys all master/slave devices such as the master slave manipulators (MSMs) used within the nuclear industry. Lastly the widely acclaimed founding father of the modern robot, Engleberger, when asked, "Can you define a robot", is reputed to have replied "No but I will recognise one when I see one". This leads us by illustration to a recognition that, although it seems straight forward, the definition of robotics, and hence the expectations of any user, may still even today differ widely.

For the purposes of this chapter, therefore, robotics is considered to be the use of computer controlled equipment to carry out work in harsh or hostile environments together with the man machine interface, peripheral sensors and other support systems required.

13.1.2 Definition of telerobotics

Following on from the above, telerobotics refers, by its title, to the use of robotics "at a distance". Since this ability has been inextricably linked to a capability to provide high fidelity feedback to the operator from the distant working place (bilateral control), it has also become synonymous with the use of advanced equipment.

13.2 Key aspects of the nuclear working environment

The nuclear working environment has many environmental and physical features which influence the application of telerobots. Some of these are primary and some are secondary. Some reflect on the life of the equipment, others on the comfort and operational capabilities of the operator.

Taken at face value, the primary factor is the presence of ionising radiation. This influences the life of the equipment and hence its design. It also precludes the use of people close to the work area and this in turn gives rise to a host of secondary inhibitions such as the need for distant working. The lack of sensory feedback caused by this dislocation leads the industry to go to extraordinary lengths to ensure that work can be carried out in a safe and effective manner.

To enable work to be carried out, the industry has, over its life time, evolved a range of operational scenarios and protective devices to accommodate these major problems implicit in handling nuclear materials. These have been typified in:

- heavy shielded walls to allow the operator to approach the work area

- shielded lead glass or zinc bromide windows to permit a direct view of the work process

- simple manual or power operated handling devices to permit the movement of materials and the execution of tasks within the work area

- the use of indirect devices such as microphones and cameras to supplement the direct sensory feedback

The methods adopted have reflected on the design of facilities. For example, the reliance on the mechanically linked MSM dictated the internal dimensions of the work cell in that, being a direct "one to one" device, replicating the operators physical reach and load carrying capacity it resulted in a relatively narrow facility (about 2 to 3 metres, front to back). Again since the work volume covered by such devices is restricted, it led to a series of small work bench areas and required a significant number of these to make up a typical cave suite. The penalties of such caves include; monolithic structures with no natural light, implicitly sound proofed, not easily changed to meet future needs. Even where some of these failings have been tackled by artificial means they still have problems. For example shield windows can lead to distortion of the view, itself leading to stress on the operator; distortion of colour, and even with the most up to date windows, a restriction in the field of view. Indirect viewing can lead to loss of orientation, scale and perception of scale and distance.

13.3 Knock-on aspects of the operational needs

Notwithstanding the direct impact of the limitations outlined above, there are several extremely significant "knock-on" effects. They are as follows:

The shape, size and materials of construction of the facility lead to high first costs. Likewise the need for foolproof equipment can also reflect adversely on the cost to produce and prove. As an example of this it should be remembered that all equipment placed into the active area must be capable of retrieval and/or repair from any conceivable fault. This in turn requires a significant cost for emergency features, many of which may never be used in anger.

Except for the more repetitive operational tasks, there is need for a high level of skill in the operators. This in turn leads to a concentration of the skills in a relatively few people. Even having highly skilled operators does not protect them from the high strain and fatigue ever-present in such operations resulting from continual interpretative viewing, shortage of sensory perception and, not insignificantly at times, an overload of information.

To achieve acceptable reliability requires that significant development and testing precedes any attempt to use the equipment operationally. In addition, for critical equipment or techniques where designs may not have been previously proven, a secondary or even tertiary development route may have to be followed to guard against failure.

All this has also to been seen alongside the inevitable need for pre-operation mock-up facilities, which have to be capable of identifying and replicating all the possible operational scenarios, both planned and emergency, and must accurately reflect the operational plant. It is not unusual to find that mock-ups built to test the complete range of possible problem areas are only needed in a small number. Conversely the more the mock-up replicates the plant, the more "permanent" its method of construction and hence the more difficult it is to reconfigure equipment layouts etc. after the project has become fixed.

13.4 VR simulation

Before going on to discuss the ways in which simulation can aid the developer/operator it is necessary to define the way in which the descriptors are interpreted within the nuclear environment.

In its briefest form they are collectively taken to refer to the real time simulation of operational plant and the equipment and processes being carried out in them. In the context of this it is clear that VR does not refer to total immersion of the operator with tactile feedback via such devices as a data glove. Where force reflection is utilised it is experienced via a normal bilateral force feedback loop and replicated through the operator manual interface as for example with a Bilateral Stewart Platform (BSP) control device. Immersion is restricted to free placement and adjustment of the operator view point.

A key element of the total systems being developed within BNFL is the absolute requirement for real time updating of the model in its entirety. This need is driven by the somewhat special requirements of the industry which has a significant amount of work to be carried out in facilities that are not well documented in solid model form from past drawings. An additional requirement is to enable satisfactory operation of equipment within facilities that are being "changed" in real time as is the case during decommissioning.

13.5 Identification of advantages and savings

13.5.1 Pre-operation

VR simulation can provide tangible benefits in allowing "concurrent engineering" to take place. In practice this means that the usual processes of solution formulation, design preparation, component manufacture, development and testing can all be explored in the virtual environment. Of course such activities have taken place to some extent before. However they have always been restricted by the difficulties of defining and replicating the real world at the time the solutions were being conceived. Whilst good use has been made of solid modelling in the past this could not provide the feel and dynamism of the present VR simulations.

Seen in this light it is clear that the techniques can significantly aid the process of demonstrating the problem and optimisation of a solution. Another advantage is seen in its capability to provide a basis for operator training to take place in parallel with the normal project activities. Operator/driver input at this early stage can provide important feedback into the design optimisation processes where appropriate especially into areas such as potentially vexing problems.

As the preliminary investigative work is more realistic and closer to the final application it allows a clear definition to be made of the shape and content of the final hard mock-up that may be required. This area alone can lead to significant savings.

13.5.2 *In operation*

However the VR simulation capability is not restricted only to the pre-operational phases of the work. During the task it can provide a wealth of information to supplement the normal CCTV.

At one level this can simply be the ability of the system to mimic the real machines within the work area. Such information can be extremely useful to the operator allowing a three-dimensional view of the task to supplement the normal viewing equipment.

Whilst the above is obtained by linking the performance of the graphics and the real equipment including the images and viewing positions, other useful information can be obtained by using the fly-through capabilities to investigate positional clearances, viewing and lighting angles etc.

For a number of tasks where there is a large amount of complex manipulation required to access or exit from a work area, it should be possible to use the model to investigate the routing, either manually or by automatic route planning techniques, thereafter downloading the sequence to the in-cell equipment for "automatic" repetition. In the case of pre-planned work such route determination may well have come from the mock-up work or even the original simulations.

13.5.3 *Post-operation*

The uses of these techniques are not restricted to the pre-operational and operational phases. Significant information can be gained from post-operational analysis of the recorded data. In the worst scenario this may have the same function as the flight recorder on an aircraft, allowing faults and problems in operation to be more fully investigated. However, the more usual use for such data would be to post-analyse the successful process with the aim of ensuring that all relevant experience was identified, captured and made available for future operations.

Within the nuclear industry it is increasingly the case that advanced teleoperated equipment has, and must be seen to have, an extended life to balance the heavy capital investment involved in its procurement and support. The implications of such longevity are that operators have to be trained and retrained in its use. Unfortunately after the initial active operational phase it is usually impracticable to return the equipment to the development workshops. Such restrictions have meant that, in the past, new operators could only get their experience on the real equipment, with the attendant risks this implies. VR simulation provides a means whereby they can be trained in significant parts of the work. Again using the aircraft analogy it can provide flight simulator capability to progress new operators towards the time of their "solo flights" when inevitably they have to be in the real world. It is also practicable to give operators refresher training to both re-validate and extend their capabilities.

13.6 Future improvements

VR simulation is advancing at a fast pace. There are however two areas in which significant advances are still to be made and without which the full potential of the techniques will be difficult to realise. These areas are described in the following two sections.

13.6.1 Real time world model updating

World model updating is seen as the ability to determine the location, shape and size of objects within the working environment and to transmit these to, and incorporate them in, a solid geometric model linked to the operational equipment. To have this in real time implies an ability to carry out all operations within a cycle time of the order of one second.

This is seen as an area being critical to the successful application of the technology in the nuclear working environment where it is essential to see changes to the work place as they are being made. As mentioned earlier this applies increasingly within the decommissioning area where the whole reason for the operations being carried out is to change the shape, size and location of objects. In effect taking what might have been a structured environment and changing it into a unstructured one.

Another though less utilised reason for having this capability is to allow intervention to take place into either previously uncharted territory or into areas where the nature of the events leading to the intervention have themselves caused the environment to become unstructured.

13.6.2 Dynamic and random event modelling

Another more esoteric but nevertheless important area for concern involves the modelling of random events for such things as umbilical cable handling. Whilst present graphical systems can model the detail equipment design down to as fine a detail as one is normally prepared to go, the scope for handling dynamic performance is usually limited to pre-defined events using fairly basic dynamic theory. Unfortunately life does not always comply neatly with the theory and where problems have been experienced in the past they have usually been with the random events relating to such things as cable handling and their ability to take up positions not intended by the designer. Such excursions can and have led to cable snags, pinches and, in extreme circumstances loss of power or control.

Index